The
SPIRITUALITY
of AGE

"Are you a Boomer on a white-knuckled ride trying to shift into reverse on aging? We all try. This knowing book will relax your grip. The authors illuminate the path of spiritual growth, leading us to come to terms with where we have failed and to make the passage to what really matters. Beautifully written, both from deep research and even deeper personal experience by the authors, a former Jesuit and a Jewish woman. Best book I have ever read on this most significant passage."

GAIL SHEEHY, AUTHOR OF *DARING: MY PASSAGES*

"At last, a book about aging that does not envision it as a problem to be solved or even as a challenge to be overcome! It greets growing older, as a gift and an opportunity. With age comes at least a little wisdom, and that wisdom is relevant for people in any age cohort. I savored this fine volume and commend it to anyone still searching, as I hope we all are, for the fullness of life."

HARVEY G. COX,
HOLLIS RESEARCH PROFESSOR OF DIVINITY,
HARVARD UNIVERSITY, AND AUTHOR OF *THE FUTURE OF FAITH*

"An in-depth look within by two specialists on aging, a woman and a man, aging Boomers themselves. It portrays aging as a spiritual experience, and unlike many current commentaries about people turning away from religion—particularly those who say 'I'm spiritual but not religious'—they turn that phrase on its head. People across faith traditions as well as secularists will find the book engaging and eye-opening."

WADE CLARK ROOF, J.F. ROWNY PROFESSOR
OF RELIGION AND SOCIETY EMERITUS,
UNIVERSITY OF CALIFORNIA AT SANTA BARBARA

"This wise and lovely book invites readers to take their aging seriously and honestly as a time for growing into spiritual wisdom. The authors ask us to ponder with them 25 questions that will help us to such wisdom. They reveal themselves as they strive to answer the questions they pose and in the process draw us toward developing our own spirituality of age. Readers will, as I do, thank them for their generosity and their wisdom."

REV. WILLIAM A. BARRY, S.J.,
AUTHOR OF *PRAYING THE TRUTH:
DEEPENING YOUR FRIENDSHIP
WITH GOD THROUGH HONEST PRAYER*

"*The Spirituality of Age* fills an important gap, not by telling people what they ought to think about this subject, but by posing a large array of vital questions that can fuel the readers' own imaginations. The authors know that there is no single path to the spirituality of age and that we have to discover our own unique, energizing and motivating answers. Their modeling is eloquent, thoughtful, and useful. Time spent with this book can bring great insight and direction."

ROBERT C. ATCHLEY, PH.D., AUTHOR OF
SPIRITUALITY AND AGING

"For those of us heeding the call to spiritual deepening in our elder years, *The Spirituality of Age* is a unique resource. The questions that form the core of this inspiring book are those that many of us carry on this journey. And the rich, experience-filled responses of the coauthors as well as the exercises they suggest will be invaluable in helping readers understand the many facets of their own spiritual potential and development as they age."

RON PEVNY, DIRECTOR OF THE
CENTER FOR CONSCIOUS ELDERING AND
AUTHOR OF *CONSCIOUS LIVING, CONSCIOUS AGING*

"These days we often hear the word *spirituality*. The spiritual search is a vital and continuous area of personal reflection for these authors. They encourage each of us to define the meaning of that word for ourselves. This book opens the door for all of us to explore our own growth, insights, inner peace, and continued learning that is calling to us as we age"

CONNIE GOLDMAN, AUTHOR OF
WHO AM I NOW THAT I'M NOT WHO I WAS?

"All of us get older, few of us get wiser. As we search for an 'authentic' spiritual practice we ignore the one we were given when we were born: aging. *The Spirituality of Age* places you firmly on this path. This is a book to be read, but more importantly lived."

RABBI RAMI SHAPIRO, AUTHOR OF
PERENNIAL WISDOM FOR THE SPIRITUALLY INDEPENDENT

"The authors are compassionate guides on the journey of aging. They beckon the reader to face the path ahead with honesty and courage. Through their own hard-won wisdom, they shine a light of hope for all of us who will, sooner or later, leave health, illusion, and life itself behind."

RABBI DAYLE A. FRIEDMAN, FOUNDER OF GROWING OLDER
AND AUTHOR OF *JEWISH WISDOM FOR GROWING OLDER*

"The authors have created a masterpiece! This book is a must-read for all facing the quest for meaning and purpose in later life. With their honest, profound, and often witty point-counterpoint perspectives on 25 of the major challenges of the gift of years, this book will enrich and deepen the lives of all of its readers and will be especially helpful to those guiding older adults on the path of psycho-spiritual growth in the second half of life. I am buying copies for all of my over-50 friends for Christmas!"

JANE M. THIBAULT, PH.D.,
CLINICAL GERONTOLOGIST AND PROFESSOR EMERITA,
UNIVERSITY OF LOUISVILLE SCHOOL OF MEDICINE

"This little book, built around questions to which each of us will have different and individual answers, emphasizes by its very structure that in our era, old age can be a time of growth and spiritual discovery, a time of fulfillment of life, rather than its dreary aftermath."

MARY CATHERINE BATESON,
CULTURAL ANTHROPOLOGIST AND
AUTHOR OF *COMPOSING A FURTHER LIFE*

"The authors have penned an exceptionally wise and timely book. Wrestling with the hard spiritual questions that so often disturb our later years, they dig deep for personal answers and generously encourage the reader to do the same. Get ready, you may find yourself revising everything you think about aging and in the process making peace with your own answers. Perfect for personal growth, book clubs, and classes."

JOHN C. ROBINSON, PH.D., D.MIN.,
PSYCHOLOGIST, INTERFAITH MINISTER, AND
AUTHOR OF *THE THREE SECRETS OF AGING*

"To my delight, this book prompted me to ask questions of myself that I had never posed before with so much clarity. The authors each respond to these questions themselves, a unique approach that is not ponderous or heavy-handed. I found myself leaving the safety of reader-as-spectator and entering the provocation of reader-as-participant. My own spiritual inquiry began to breathe more freshly."

WENDY LUSTBADER, MSW,
AUTHOR OF *LIFE GETS BETTER:
THE UNEXPECTED PLEASURES OF GROWING OLDER*

The
SPIRITUALITY
of AGE

A Seeker's Guide
to Growing Older

ROBERT L. WEBER, Ph.D.,
and CAROL ORSBORN, Ph.D.

Park Street Press
Rochester, Vermont • Toronto, Canada

Park Street Press
One Park Street
Rochester, Vermont 05767
www.ParkStPress.com

SUSTAINABLE FORESTRY INITIATIVE

Certified Sourcing
www.sfiprogram.org
SFI-00854

Text stock is SFI certified

Park Street Press is a division of Inner Traditions International

Scripture quotations are from the New Revised Standard Version Bible, copyright © 1989 the Division of Christian Education of the National Council of the Churches of Christ in the United States of America. Used by permission. All rights reserved.

"The Guest House" by Rumi reprinted by permission of Coleman Barks, translator.

"Prayer for the Grace to Age Well" by Teilhard de Chardin used with permission: © The Institute of Jesuit Sources at the Institiute for Advanced Jesuit Studies, Boston College, Chestnut Hill, MA. All rights reserved.

Some of Carol Orsborn's essays are retellings of stories or insights shared in her blogs. Her blog sites are listed in "About the Authors" on pages 229–30.

Library of Congress Cataloging-in-Publication Data
Weber, Robert L.
 The spirituality of age : a seeker's guide to growing older / Robert L. Weber, Carol Orsborn.
  pages cm
 Summary: "A compassionate guide for transforming aging into spiritual growth"— Provided by publisher.
 Includes bibliographical references.
 ISBN 978-1-62055-512-5 (paperback) — ISBN 978-1-62055-513-2 (ebook)
 1. Self-realization in old age. 2. Older people—Conduct of life. 3. Aging— Religious aspects. I. Orsborn, Carol. II. Title.
 BF724.85.S45W43 2015
 155.67'19—dc23
                                                           2015009187

Printed and bound in the United States by Lake Book Manufacturing, Inc.
The text stock is SFI certified. The Sustainable Forestry Initiative® program promotes sustainable forest management.

10 9 8 7 6 5 4 3 2 1

Text design by Debbie Glogover and layout by Priscilla Baker
This book was typeset in Garamond Premier Pro, with Granjon and Futura used as display typefaces

*To our irrepressible generation of seekers, so many
of whom are joining us in making the leap to
aging not only as a spiritual path
but as a mystical experience*

Note to Readers

We welcome readers of all traditions, faiths, beliefs, and communities to this book, and hope you will use our responses to these twenty-five seminal questions as a springboard to connect with your own source of guidance and inspiration. As both coauthors grew up within belief systems that were God-centered, our responses to the questions often naturally refer to the Divine as "God," using the terminology that is most meaningful to us. However, we recognize that many of our readers may see themselves as being "spiritual, but not religious." This book is also for you. Our use of "the Divine" and similar terms in the introductory sections is meant to provide you with an open-ended invitation to enter into a more intimate relationship with that which ultimately transcends all definition.

Contents

PART II
25 QUESTIONS
A Journey of Spiritual Inquiry

⑥

Appendix

Twelve Exercises for Seekers 189

☉

Summons to a Leap of Faith

Harry R. Moody, Ph.D.

Aging, as we all know, comes whether we like it or not. If consciously accepted, our sense that time is short, and many important questions are yet to be answered, can be a moment of "Call": a wake-up message summoning us to what is deepest and most authentic in us. This is the "going home" Call that some of us who are not only aging, but aging consciously, are fortunate indeed to hear.

Not everyone does, and some of those who hear the Call just press the snooze-alarm and go back to sleep: "Yes, I'll get to that when I'm retired" or "Some questions just don't have answers" and so on.

But if the question, "How shall I live?" becomes pressing, even irresistible, then we move into the next stage of our soul's evolution, when we recognize that we need guidance, we need a map. In its most elemental form, we need to know that we're not crazy. We need to talk to others who have gone through a similar process if we're to find the guidance that we need.

This is where *The Spirituality of Age* becomes a vital source of help. What coauthors Bob Weber and Carol Orsborn have brought to their new book is the summons to a leap of faith, a moment of awakening that calls upon us to take responsibility for our lives. As *The Spirituality of Age* demonstrates, valid guidance, good guidance, doesn't take away from the seeker the responsibility and freedom to choose, to make judgments, to find the path that is distinctively one's own.

But this is sometimes easier said than done. When we receive the Call in later life, we will soon find ourselves in a "supermarket" of bewildering choices: go to the self-help section of the bookstore, fire up your Kindle, start cruising the Internet, get the Road Scholar catalog, visit the churches or the psychotherapists, talk to friends and other seekers. Just writing this list is exhausting. Trying to live it, and make good choices, is impossible—unless, unless, we have guidance.

Here is where, again, *The Spirituality of Age* becomes indispensable. The coauthors teach us that we become wise, if and only if we learn to love the questions. Like Socrates, their wisdom derives from the transparency of their own questions and the restraint with which they refrain from imposing their conclusions on others. What remains consistent throughout is their recognition of the centrality of the spiritual quest—by which I mean the search for meaning—in later life. And this recognition is the understanding that "successful aging" must be more than simply adding new birthdays or simply repeating the steps that helped us get through life so far. In other words, truly "successful aging" is aging that comes with questions about what "success" means in the first place.

In their first chapter the authors cite Rilke's advice:

Be patient toward all that is unsolved in your heart and try to love the questions themselves, like locked rooms and like books that are now written in a very foreign tongue. Do not now seek the answers, which cannot be given you because you would not be able to live them. And the point is, to live everything. Live the questions now. Perhaps you will then gradually, without noticing it, live along some distant day into the answer.[1]

Rilke wrote these wise words in his *Letters to a Young Poet*. But his guidance is equally applicable to later life, with this important qualification: we cannot anticipate that we will "gradually, without noticing it" live the answers in "some distant day." The clock is ticking, and the distant day must be now, or very soon. Writing this on the eve of my seventieth birthday, I am acutely aware that none of us can know how much time we have.

So guidance to the seeker means calling our attention to this fundamental truth: the Call and the Search reach fruition not in "peace of mind" but in the Struggle. This Struggle—that "something else" we must each bring to not only age, but age wisely—is the subject of this wonderful book. Readers are indeed fortunate to find here the guidance they're seeking. For the reader who is ready to dig in, *The Spirituality of Age* will become an indispensable map.

HARRY R. MOODY is Distinguished Visiting Professor, Creative Longevity and Wisdom Program, Fielding Graduate University, as well as emeritus director of Academic Affairs and Vice President for AARP.

He is the author of numerous books and articles including the classic *The Five Stages of the Soul.*

His other titles include: *Abundance of Life: Human Development Policies for an Aging Society, Ethics in an Aging Society,* and *Aging: Concepts and Controversies,* a gerontology textbook now in its eighth edition.

A graduate of Yale and holder of a Ph.D. in philosophy from Columbia University, Harry Moody taught philosophy at Columbia, Hunter College, New York University, and the University of California at Santa Cruz.

From 1999 to 2001 he served as National Program Director of the Robert Wood Johnson Foundation's Faith in Action and, from 1992 to 1999, was executive director of the Brookdale Center at Hunter College. Before coming to Hunter he served as administrator of Continuing Education Programs for the Citicorp Foundation and later as codirector of the National Aging Policy Center of the National Council on Aging in Washington, D.C.

Harry Moody is known nationally for his work in older adult education and served as Chairman of the Board of Elderhostel.

Acknowledgments

We are very grateful to the following individuals and groups whose relationships with us began to birth this book many years ago.

BOB WEBER

My wife and my best friend, Pamela Enders, whose loving heart and depth of mind and spirit enthrall me and give me a profound appreciation that love is the centerpiece and anchor of our existence. She continually opens my eyes to the truth about myself and the reality of God's love in the world. Her presence in my life is "the present of presents!"

My dad and mom, Louis and Mary, who brought me into the world, loved me, and nurtured me so that I could become more and more who I am. I thank my dad especially for seeding the gifts of gratitude, forgiveness, and tears into my young heart and the spirit of perpetual childlikeness. My mom gave me a sense of unwavering, nonhovering presence. Her own experience of suffering heartens me now as aging brings on suffering of various kinds, and her response to me in the face of my early fears of death endowed me with courage not to deny the reality, but to face it and live most fully.

My sister, Gerri, and my brother, Gene: their presence in my life has helped me and continues to help me grow in my capacity to love them and to live in community with them and other brothers and sisters in the world, while not avoiding the inevitable conflicts that require time to heal and growth to occur.

The Society of Jesus and its many members, the Jesuits, who nurtured my spirituality through their friendship, direction, and encouragement, and who gave me the freedom to become more truly who I am.

The American Society on Aging and the Forum on Religion, Spirituality, and Aging for providing a community in which I have been welcomed and encouraged to weave together three important strands of my personal and professional life: mental health, aging, and spirituality. This book is the fruit of my efforts at weaving.

And finally, what a privilege and gift to coauthor this book with Carol Orsborn! She brought the riches of her mind, heart, and spirit to me and to our work. Her contagious energy and enthusiasm infused all of our conversations. May our friendship and collaboration continue for years to come!

CAROL ORSBORN

As always, my heartfelt thanks to Dan, my family, and friends who give my life, heart, and words wings.

To contributors and readers of *Fierce with Age, the Digest of Boomer Wisdom, Inspiration and Spirituality,* as well as participants in my Fierce with Age retreats. This formerly lone ranger loves getting off her horse and splashing around in the ever-growing pond of the conscious aging movement and its epicenter: The Conscious Aging Alliance.

A particular shout-out to my coauthor Bob Weber. I can think of no better conversation partner on this journey through the wild side of midlife. You inspire me and make me laugh, often at the same time. A rare and precious combination!

In Memoriam: My beloved spiritual guide and friend Diane Caughey, Ph.D.

My gratitude to you all is fierce, indeed.

THE COAUTHORS

This book would not have been made possible without the encouragement and aid of our professional peers and crackerjack publication team.

Our gratitude to Rick Moody and Andy Achenbaum for your early and ongoing support of our vision for *The Spirituality of Age.* Thank you for your thoughtful, encouraging foreword and afterword.

To the American Society of Aging and Alison Biggar of *Aging Today,* for allowing us such a prestigious platform from which to float our cornerstone thesis in our article: "The Question(s) of Age: Calling for a New Vision of Spiritual Aging," published in *Aging Today* in March–April 2013.

Linda Roghaar, literary agent extraordinaire, for helping us craft our original concept into something publishable— and finding exactly the right home for it. We value your honesty, your knowledge, your vision, your persistence, and your faith.

Last but not least, we cannot say enough great things about the publishing team at Inner Traditions/Park Street Press: Jon Graham, acquisitions editor; Jeanie Levitan, editor in chief; Nancy Yielding, our line editor; our marketing team, especially

Manzanita Carpenter and director of sales, John Hays; and the book's interior designer, Debbie Glogover, and cover designer, Peri Swan. And a special shout-out to Laura Schlivek, our project editor at Inner Traditions. We hope you are pleased when we acknowledge each of you with our highest praise: "You are one of us."

PART I

⊚

CALLING FOR A
NEW VISION OF
SPIRITUAL AGING

The Guest House

This being human is a guest house.
Every morning a new arrival.

A joy, a depression, a meanness,
some momentary awareness comes
As an unexpected visitor.

Welcome and entertain them all!
Even if they're a crowd of sorrows,
who violently sweep your house
empty of its furniture,
still treat each guest honorably.
He may be clearing you out
for some new delight.

The dark thought, the shame, the malice,
meet them at the door laughing,
and invite them in.

Be grateful for whoever comes,
because each has been sent
as a guide from beyond.

RUMI
FROM *THE ESSENTIAL RUMI*,
TRANSLATED BY COLEMAN BARKS

Aging as the Path to Spiritual Maturity

Once we hit midlife and beyond, the dominant societal formulations of aging present us with three choices. The first, and the one that influences all the others, either consciously or unconsciously, is that it is our destiny to become increasingly marginalized and disengaged as we grow older, a sad slow decline. This is the notion that sends dread into the aging boomer's heart.

The second more popular stance regarding aging is complete denial: old age is simply an extension of a never-ending midlife. Turn to any magazine, and you will see this in every antiaging tagline that promises "fifty is the new thirty." Don't like the idea of aging? Just don't do it.

The third choice, a variation of denial, grows from seeds deeply rooted in contemporary academic theories about aging. This positive view of successful aging advocates old age as a time to be filled with activity and productivity. This is the vision of aging that drives everything from the reinvention movement to articles exalting ninety-year-old role models for running marathons and starting new businesses. A romanticized version of this positive view of aging, often dressed up in spiritual jargon, likewise white-washes the shadow side of growing older, promising aging to be a time of wisdom, serenity, and peace.

A growing number of us transiting the new and challenging territory of midlife and beyond reject all these formulations. In their place we increasingly share a fourth vision of aging that beckons us to take into account both the light and the shadow side of growing old. Admittedly, establishing and maintaining both a hopeful and realistic vision of the aging process requires a level of spiritual maturity that challenges the best of us. But this is the only path to embracing the entirety of our lives as the fulfillment of our spiritual purpose.

When we, the coauthors of this book, speak about the challenge of advancing to a new level of spiritual maturity, we are not just speaking theoretically. In fact, this book was birthed out of just such a moment of transition, a chance encounter that demonstrates three of the major premises of this book: (1) that spiritual growth and opportunity can come to us when we least expect it, whether we feel we are deserving of it or not; (2) that such moments of divine intervention can come about not only despite the challenges that aging has thrust upon us, but because of them; and (3) that the Divine is both mysterious and loving.

THE BIRTH OF THIS BOOK

The initiation of this book began on a stairwell landing in San Francisco in the spring of 2011. Rick Moody and Bob Weber had just finished a standing-room-only presentation for the Forum on Religion, Spirituality, and Aging at the Annual Meeting of the American Society on Aging (ASA). The presentation was entitled "Aging as a Natural Monastery: A Time for ContemplAgeing," a presentation title that was the fruit of Bob's dialogue and work with Dr. Jane Marie Thibault. Carol Orsborn, who had just completed a presentation of her own on the subject of the stages of adult development and boomer women, had been in the audience, drawn to the topic for personal as well as professional reasons.

From the moment she'd crossed the threshold into the hotel lobby, Carol had intuited that somehow this ASA would be different from those she'd spoken at in the past. For starters, after years of attending as an aging expert, but not someone who actually considered herself to be in the demographic, she realized with some sense of shock that the thousands of older men and women who crowded into the lobby were actually her peers. She was no longer the younger outsider providing expert counsel on "older women." In fact, at the 2011 ASA, it was suddenly apparent to her that the boomer generation was not in attendance only as experts, policy makers, salespeople, institutional leaders, support professionals, caregivers, and do-gooders. We were also there because we wanted something for ourselves.

Many of the seekers in attendance had, like Carol, been drawn to the description of Rick and Bob's presentation in the program: "Aging is a time for an entering into the sacred space of the unique circumstances of your own aging in a contemplative way. This session will view aging from these perspectives, envisioning it as a time to enhance spiritual growth, deepen spiritual life and practice, and expand the fullness of life." Deeply moved by the presentation, Carol sat thoughtfully in the meeting room as the exuberant participants filed out and the next group and topic drifted in. Eventually, she found her way to the stairs in the hall outside, not sure whether to go up or down, nor where she was headed.

It was there, on the first landing between floors, thousands of people swarming above and below, Carol and Bob bumped into each other. The surprise and synchronicity of the moment inspired the initiation of a conversation that continued on the landing for over an hour, spilling over into an ongoing dialogue that ultimately resulted in the book you now hold in your hands.

Parallel Journeys

It became immediately apparent that the two of us had each been on our own different but parallel spiritual journeys, spurred on by our own aging and the hunger to find meaning in the second half of our lives. Additionally, we each had felt a degree of loneliness in our efforts to embrace not only the possibilities of aging, but the shadow side as well. During that first conversation we established that we felt something was missing, not only at ASA, but in most of the spiritual support systems related to aging we had found available. We decided to pool resources and embark on a mutual exploration of the possibilities. In the early weeks and months, we found our conversations healing and rejuvenating, and that would have been enough.

But eventually, gradually, we both began to recognize that the questions we were asking of one another, the issues we were addressing, and the processes that we were co-creating, to such mutually beneficial results, together represented something that we should share with others. Of course, this didn't come completely out of the blue, as we have both written and spoken professionally about matters of the heart over the decades. Nevertheless, our realization that we could take learnings from our private journeys about spirituality and aging public came as a pleasant surprise to us both: the integration of our professional aptitudes and proclivities with the deepest calling of our spirits.

Going Public

The joy of this book comes not only out of private introspection, but even more out of the rejuvenating, and often challenging, dialogue between companions and peers. While it often feels as though we share the same sense of the Divine working in our lives, we bring divergent—while synergistic—backgrounds to this project. Bob is a former Jesuit; Carol grew up Jewish. Bob is a male, and Carol is a female. Bob is a trained clinical psychologist; Carol's credential is a doctorate in the history and critical theory of religion. We have individual but increasingly overlapping circles of influence. But above all we have the same sense of mission: the urge to share our spiritual process and discoveries as we transit from midlife into older age, and to invite others into the dialogue.

We made our debut with the questions that form the basis for this book at the Fifth Annual Positive Aging Conference in Los Angeles on the topic: "Developing Resilience through Spiritual Exercise in the Second Half of Life" about one year after our first meeting. Shortly thereafter, we were invited to write a provocative article, now incorporated into this book, titled "The Question(s) of Age: Calling for a New Vision of Spiritual Aging." The article appeared in *Aging Today*, the American Society of Aging's influential publication. The positive response to our growing body of work, including speeches, interviews, articles, and blogs, have reinforced our conviction that we are onto something important that is of service to others.

THE NEED FOR A NEW VISION
OF SPIRITUAL AGING

Our yearning for a spirituality of age that would consider both the light and shadow sides of life at midlife and beyond finds its roots in recent gerontological history.* In the 1960s and 1970s, the two predominant theories of aging that emerged in the field of gerontology were "disengagement" and "activity."[1]

Disengagement theory purports that an inevitable and mutually agreed upon withdrawal between the individual and society occurs as old age approaches.[2] This mutual withdrawal or disengagement is seen as a developmental process, universal in its occurrence, with implications for the successful maintenance of the society and for the individual's adjustment in regard to morale. According to the theory, with disengagement there is no loss of morale since a new level of equilibrium is reached in terms of social interaction.

Activity theory, on the other hand, maintains that adjustment to old age is dependent on a high activity level, especially in terms of social interactions and social role participation.[3] From this perspective disengagement is viewed as being forced on the elderly person by sociocultural conditions rather than chosen.[4]

These two perspectives have had a major influence in gerontological circles, while other viewpoints about aging continue to emerge, in great part because we are living longer and the realities of aging are more apparent to the American culture. While

---

*Gerontology is a field of study that covers social, psychological, biological, and cognitive dimensions of aging. While it is related to geriatrics, the latter is an area of specialization treating the diseases of older adults as a branch of medicine.

there are a few notable exceptions, such as the new conscious aging movement, the majority of theories are accompanied by an overarching and unwelcoming stance to growing older—a kind of "denial of death" as Ernst Becker wrote well before this era.[5]

Certainly, there are reasons why we, as a culture, would choose to avoid such harsh and unwelcome realities of aging as physical diminishment, erosion of valued social roles, losses of our loved ones, and endings of familiar ways of being in the world. Theologian Henri Nouwen, in his prescient book published forty years ago, *Aging: The Fulfillment of Life,* described trends in our culture regarding aging including segregation, desolation, and loss of self-respect.[6] More recently, Susan Jacoby wrote on similar themes in *Never Say Die: The Myth and Marketing of the New Old Age.* This book corroborates our experience that there is a powerful "antiaging" cultural trend afoot that has given birth to an antiaging industry, which promotes "the new old age" while avoiding discussion of "the real old age."[7] For most of us the real old age is not and will not be a discovery of the fountain of youth.

Not long ago, while still offering her services to major brands as one of the premiere experts on marketing to boomer women, Carol had experienced the same ethos of antiaging sentiment at play in both advertising and the media. In a youth-obsessed society, aspirational messaging did not aim to motivate one to become one's personal best, but rather, to act, think, and look like someone decades younger. If the aging individual in question wasn't climbing a mountain, dressing in the same clothes as her daughter, surveying her vineyard, or quietly slinking off into the sunset hand-in-hand with her Viagra-fueled spouse, many marketers acted as if this consumer wasn't worth marketing to.

A Holistic View

There is nothing wrong with wanting to stay as youthful, active, and positive as possible. If you have the wherewithal to remain active, by all means do so! The wisdom and experience of a life lived into old age can and must serve the culture, suffusing it with the vital generativity and ego integrity (wisdom) that life stage expert Erik Erikson describes.*[8]

What is problematic, however, is skewing and distorting a full picture of aging and denying the other opportunities that are inherent in the aging process. So, what is the nature of these opportunities? This is the valuing of the spiritual potential of aging that is too infrequently given full voice in the professional world of gerontology. Even if it is not completely absent, it is certainly underexpressed. This underrepresented vision of aging is the opportunity to grow spiritually throughout the course of our lives that is part and parcel of our growing older, the breakthrough understanding that comprises the heart and soul of this book's mission.

Admittedly, not everyone understands and endorses our commitment to embrace the shadow as well as the light side of aging, leaving nothing out, including illness, decline, and mortality, while still doing everything possible for an ongoing life of fulfillment. "Living life to the full" has its challenges. As

---

*According to Erickson generativity is a concern for people besides self and family that usually develops during middle age. This concern manifests especially as the urge to nurture and guide younger people and contribute to the next generation (Merriam-Webster online). Ego integrity is the peak of his eight stages of psychosocial development. He wrote that "for the fruit of these seven stages I know no better word than ego integrity . . . the ego's accrued assurance of its proclivity for order and meaning" (Erikson, *Childhood and Society,* 259–60).

T. S. Eliot wrote, "Human kind cannot bear very much reality."[9] Perhaps that is why, especially when it comes to aging, the tendency is to go into denial and stop asking ourselves the important questions. Questions are born in the midst of confusion, uncertainty, and unpredictability, and we do not like to live in the midst of such conditions. We want clarity, certainty, and predictability. We are even willing to settle for lies that mask as truth, rather than face the deeper existential questions that are unavoidable. The poet Rainer Maria Rilke had a correspondence with a young man who agonized over whether he should be a poet. Rilke responded, "This above all—ask yourself in the stillest hour of your night; must I write? Delve into yourself for a deep answer." Rilke invited the man to enter his own "dark night" and ask himself the most important question he was facing at the time, "must I write [?]"[10]

This is the equivalent of what we are inviting our readers to do with us: to enter the "dark night of aging"; to not avoid the questions; and to not settle for easy answers. Rather we hope our readers will follow Rilke's counsel: "Delve into yourself for a deep answer."

Like Rilke we say to our readers, "[We] want to beg you as much as [we] can . . . to be patient toward all that is unsolved in your heart and to try to love the questions themselves. . . . Do not now seek answers which cannot be given you, because you would not be able to live them. And the point is to live everything. Live the questions now. Perhaps you will then gradually, without noticing it, live along some distant day into the answer . . . take whatever comes with great trust, and if only it comes out of your own will, out of some need of your innermost being, take it upon yourself and hate nothing."[11]

Our Hope for Our Readers

Gary Larson drew a wonderful cartoon of an art gallery proprietor, sitting in his welcoming chair. On the walls are paintings, all hung askew, tilted to the right. When you look at the owner once again, you see that his head is also tilted to the right, so all the works are hung on the level from his cockeyed perspective.[12]

It is our hope that our readers will re-view their perception of aging and perceive new realities and new possibilities inherent in aging itself. By journeying with us through this book, we will co-create a grounding for not only looking at the "too much reality" of Eliot, but also finding that we can bear it. We trust that you will have your vision of aging altered for the better, not by excluding any of the realities, but by including all and seeing yourself differently when you look in the mirror and behold the older person before you. We hope you experience our vision of aging as rooted in experiences not unlike your own, even if not precisely the same—a vision that is grounded in a mature spirituality, whatever the religious tradition or spiritual practice.

Until now aging has been unwelcome for the vast majority of us. When we begin to hear it knocking on the door of our life, we try to secure the lock and bar the door, using whatever means possible to do so. If we were instead to follow the counsel of Rumi, we would begin to see aging as another unexpected visitor to the guest house of our humanity. Rumi says we should invite all the unexpected and unwanted guests in and get to know them, even those "dark thoughts" they may create.

Welcome and entertain them all!
Even if they're a crowd of sorrows,
who violently sweep your house

empty of its furniture,
still treat each guest honorably.
He may be clearing you out
for some new delight.[13]

Hope, here, is the operative word. It is an increase of hope in light of reality that we wish above all for our readers. Hope is not "a pie in the sky" phenomenon. Hope is born and cultivated in the midst of life's messiness, in which aging plays a leading role. It is not by escaping the harsh realities that hope is birthed; it is by entering deeply into the finitude of our existence with all that implies, including suffering and death.

In his book, *Christ and Apollo: The Dimensions of the Literary Imagination,* William F. Lynch, SJ, calls this the "generative finite"—the ground in which we must be rooted in order to prosper, not just survive.[14] This new vision of the spirituality of age will enable us to open up novel possibilities for transformation of our relationship to ourselves, to others, and to the basis for meaning in our lives. It will also allow us to provide support for the spiritual lives of those for whom we care. And all of this will come about not despite the new challenges we face beyond midlife, but because of them.

2

Our Spiritual Biographies

In the back of the book, you will find the authors' formal biographies, including titles, positions, and credentials. But our résumés only tell a small part of the story. Before you dive into the heart of the book, we think introductions of a different sort are in order. By sharing our spiritual biographies with you early on, it is our hope that you will recognize us as fellow travelers on the journey to spiritual maturity.

Contemplative Aging: Living Life to the Full
Robert L. Weber, Ph.D.

My journey began postpartum in 1946—yes, I am a "baby boomer"—with baptism in the Roman Catholic Church. In the pre–Vatican II Catholic culture of the 1940s and 1950s, when I was growing up, no greater role than entering the priesthood could be conceived. So, eventually, after finishing college at Princeton University and a year of graduate school at Harvard, I entered the New England Province of the Society of Jesus, a religious order of the Church known as the Jesuits, founded in the mid-1500s by Ignatius of Loyola.

For ten years I lived, worked, and trained as a Jesuit with the intention of ordination. My ordination day would have occurred in June of 1975. However, doubts arose; with good spiritual direction, I took a leave of absence to discern whether a vocation to the priesthood was my path. Gradually, I made the decision to leave, after I had begun a doctoral program in clinical psychology at Temple University in Philadelphia. Subsequently, I married, moved back to Boston for a predoctoral internship and postdoctoral fellowship at Massachusetts General Hospital-Harvard Medical School, and launched a fruitful and fulfilling career as a psychologist in the 1980s.

Then, in the mid-1990s, my preoccupation focused more intensely on my spiritual life, a life that was rooted in my Jesuit training and the spiritual exercises of St. Ignatius.[1] That focus, when I was in my mid-fifties, included an increased awareness of my own aging and death. As a result my career path took a turn, and I became profoundly interested in the integration of three major threads of my life: my work as a psychologist, the spiritual life, and aging.

A longtime friend and colleague, Richard B. Griffin, then in his late seventies, who had been involved in gerontology as a journalist, suggested I attend my first American Society of Aging (ASA) meeting. He also encouraged me to meet Dr. Jane Marie Thibault, a professor of gerontology at the University of Louisville Medical School. She had been working for many years integrating aging, spirituality, and gerontology. I became active with ASA's Forum on Religion and Spirituality and Aging (FORSA) and was encouraged to join its Leadership Council. In 2011 I was invited to give a FORSA Featured Day presentation at ASA, where I met Carol Orsborn for the first time. In 2014 I was the recipient of the American Society on Aging's FORSA Religion and Spirituality Award, which recognizes "individuals, programs, and services in religion, spirituality, and aging."

My entrance into the professional world of gerontology began in graduate school in 1978. I studied with Dr. Diana Woodruff, a professor and protégée of Dr. James Birren, a preeminent gerontologist at the University of Southern California, where she completed her doctoral degree in gerontology. Spurred on by her teaching and excited by my studies with her, I chose to write my master's thesis in psychology on "Value Changes and Adjustment in the Elderly."

Little did I know that this would forecast my current interest, which also looks at the changes and adjustments that occur as we age. At the time, too, little did I know that my choice of this focus was motivated by a greater awareness of my parents' aging and mortality and that it was an unconscious, counterphobic reaction to these realities.

Ironically, six years after I completed my master's and doctoral degrees, on April 12, 1984, my father died suddenly, the day before I was to sit for my licensing exam in psychology. In a very real sense, I was moving ahead in my life, officially becoming a psychologist, "over my father's dead body."

I attribute some of my ease with aging and death to my upbringing in a small town Catholic culture where I was not shielded from aging and death's reality. I recall visiting my neighbor, Mr. Peter Grober, laid out in his coffin in his living room in the house next door. I remember standing graveside as an altar boy when coffins were still lowered while family and friends watched and, on occasion, attempted to jump in after a deceased mother.

The most grounding experience occurred when I was seven years old and became profoundly aware that my mother and father would die. The realization caused me to become depressed for several weeks. My mother noticed my dark mood and asked, "What's wrong?" to which I, the scared, tough little boy said, "Nothin'!" Finally, one day she encouraged me to tell her, and I blurted out, amid deep, deep sobs and tears, "You're gonna die! You're gonna die!"

She put her hand on my shoulder and assured me that, yes, she would die one day "but, probably not for a while." Then, slowly and quietly, she added, "So, in the meantime, why don't you go out and play with your friends?" My mood shifted in that moment, and I did go out to play with my friends—and I have continued to do so ever since.

My mother's gift to me was this: Go out and live, now, in the face of death, denying myself neither life nor death. My hope in writing this book is that others may discover the opportunities for life in the face of death, and relate to death not as a morbid and discouraging reality, but a life-giving one.

There is a certain irony in my life. While a Jesuit, a member of the Society of Jesus, I was unsure what I believed about Jesus Christ. I could not at the time make a confession of faith that would have reflected the creed of the Catholic Church. However, within the past ten years, this image of God, more than Father and Spirit, who predominated earlier, has become the pivotal focus of my faith. In large part this is because he was incarnated, en-fleshed like every one of us, thereby experiencing life as we know it, live it, suffer it, and die to it.

On Becoming Fierce with Age
Carol Orsborn, Ph.D.

In the Jewish tradition a child is given a Hebrew name at birth, which mystics believe will help determine the course of one's life. I have always considered it apocryphal that my Hebrew name Chai means "Life" and my middle name stands for "Joy." From as early as I can recall, I believed that my name was my birthright and that I would devote myself to clearing any obstacles that get in the way, not only for me, but for everybody in the world. Obviously, this was a tall order, and so my life has been equally devoted to pursuing the joys of life, and coming to terms with the disappointments and setbacks.

My early childhood was both joyful and shadowed. A baby boomer, like Bob, I remember hiding under my kindergarten desk in an atomic bomb drill. My father was a physician who brought his work home with him, so dinner conversation centered frequently around diseases and maladies too onerous to be named, especially the big one: "C," which took a young cousin of mine at an early age. Rather than feeling repelled by the forbidden language, I was fascinated. This explains, perhaps, the beeline I always made when going to my favorite museum: the Museum of Science and Industry in Chicago. Somewhere, hidden away in an obscure corner was a life-sized tableau of a young girl on her deathbed. The physician held her hand, helpless in the days before penicillin to save her. Her mother sat in a chair, crying, and the music that played over the loudspeaker was Beethoven's *Moonlight Sonata*.

Perhaps what saved me from morbidity was my father's larger-than-life sense of humor and the joy that he took from being alive. The story that best captures my dad's spirit centers on World War II. Dad was serving as a doctor on the front lines in the Philippines when he, himself, succumbed to malaria. The medics laid him out on a cot in a tent with many others as Dad's feverish mind put him into a delirious state. As the enemy advanced the tent was hastily disassembled and the occupants moved to safety. Except for one. In the panic of the move, my father had been left behind, left lying alone on a cot in the middle of a battlefield. Helpless, he did the one thing he could think of to give himself the best odds for survival: he began to laugh. He remembers lying there in that field, rolling in ironic joy over the foibles of life, and the predicament of the limitations of what it means to be human. Eventually the medics remembered Dad, came to retrieve him, and he was saved to live out the rest of his life to the age of ninety. Dad never stopped laughing, and it is to him that I owe my simultaneous embrace of shadow and light.

Dedicated to fulfilling the legacy of both my name and lineage, I became a seeker, eager to learn from the masters, whatever their spiritual or religious orientation. The University of California, Berkeley, in the 1960s was a magnet for alternative spirituality, and as a student, I was in the audience to hear everybody from the Dalai Lama and Swami Muktananda, to Rabbi Shlomo Carlbach and Maharishi Mahesh Yogi. On my breaks I traveled to places like Switzerland, where I sat at the feet of Krishnamurti, or to Northern California where I went on silent retreat at the Green Gulch Zen Buddhist Monastery. I was also active in the consciousness movement, moving in an increasingly spiritual progression through EST to Actualizations and finally to Temenos.

Meanwhile, I made my living as a marketer, founding my first public relations agency in 1971. But I could not help but notice the discrepancy between what I was learning about how

to live a full, joyful life, and how most of the people I encountered in my everyday work life were going about it. I, too, of
course, found that there can be a wide gap between theory and
practice, so I began keeping a journal of the challenges I faced,
and my learnings along the way. In my late thirties I had the
opportunity to take my private observations public through the
first of what became a series of books—twenty-five to date—
that comprised the heart of my spiritual practice: engaging in
discernment through the written word.

I wrote and published my first ten books about spirituality
and quality-of-life advice for boomers before deciding that a formal education in religion would be a useful thing to have. With
my husband and children's support, I enrolled in the divinity
school at Vanderbilt University where I pursued and achieved
my master's of theological studies. While attending I researched
and wrote my eleventh book: *The Art of Resilience: 100 Paths to
Wisdom and Strength in an Uncertain World*. At the time I had
already transited through a number of spiritual formulations that
I had found incapable of standing up to the real-world challenges
of life. Positive thinking, for instance, especially interpretations
that lead you to believe that if only you try hard enough, you
can control everything that happens to you. I resolved to write
a book that would stand up to any circumstance, no matter how
unwanted or threatening.

The irony is that shortly after writing the book, and before
publication, I was diagnosed with breast cancer "out of the blue."
In fact, I received my cancer diagnosis on the very same day
that I was informed that I had been accepted into the graduate
school's doctoral program in the History and Critical Theory
of Religion. What fascinated me is how we grow and change
through all the stages of our lives. I was particularly curious as

to how we achieve spiritual maturity, the experience of "wisdom" that is so closely associated with growing older. I also wondered about the disconnect I was becoming increasingly aware of between my own growing respect for the elderly, and society's marginalization of people, especially women, at midlife and beyond. My areas of expertise, Adult Development and Ritual Studies, introduced me to the literature and research, applicable on both a personal and professional level.

Treated and healed of breast cancer, and newly minted as a Ph.D., I emerged determined to make a difference to the greatest number of people. While I enjoyed teaching ethics and leadership at places like Pepperdine, Loyola Marymount, Vanderbilt, and Georgetown, I felt that I could make the greatest impact by going back to marketing with my new reservoir of spiritual and religious knowledge. (Of course, this redirection did have something to do with the difficulty I encountered attempting to secure a tenure track position "at my age.") Not surprisingly, based on my studies in adult development, I decided to take on ageism: to do everything I could within my power to inspire mainstream society as influenced by advertisers and the media to be respectful of people through all life stages. Answering this call, my mission led me to become one of the early leading experts on marketing to the boomer generation, and women fifty plus in particular.

For the ten years following my doctorate, I wrote books on the subject, spoke at major conferences, consulted with blue chip brands, and did everything I could within my power to help popular culture embrace a healthier regard for a concept of aging that embraced the shadow as well as the light.

While I made headway in my mission, by the time I'd arrived at the 2011 ASA, I was in what I would now refer to as a high functioning state of despair. My primary client, a website that offered advice to brands on marketing to women fifty plus, had taken a decidedly antiaging turn, promoting the notion of women at midlife and beyond as a decade or more younger than their chronological age. I'd been serving as the online host for the site, which worked well enough when I was in my fifties. But the older I got, especially when I crossed the line into my sixties, the more I longed to be able to act, speak, and respect my real stage in life. I was clearly at a crossroads, personally, professionally, and spiritually, asking myself whether to push through my resistance and find a new job in the same field in which I'd already invested so much. Or to take a well-deserved time-out to reconsider the choices I'd made in the past, the changes that were being imposed on me, and my right to pay heed to my heart's yearning for something more meaningful. In brief, who was I to be, and how was I going to make the most out of the rest of my life?

When I bumped into Bob on the stairwell after his presentation on a contemplative approach to aging, deeply moved, the words came tumbling out: "I'm so glad I ran into you. I'm at a moment of personal and professional decision. I've got so much to give, so much I want to do. But it's so hard right now. There's so much resistance and effort involved. Do I owe it to myself to beat a retreat, withdraw to deepen myself spiritually and develop myself as the contemplative I know I have inside of me? Or do I push through my resistance to stay engaged in the world? I'm so confused."

Bob took this all in, listened intently, sighed deeply, then replied: "Me, too."

With these two simple words, I suddenly realized that my yearning for divine counsel was no less than my spirit and the

Sacred calling to me, ever-present and available, waiting patiently for me to come home. What's more, I wasn't alone.

This book that you now hold in your hands is testimony to the fact that it is possible to take the time to ask yourself the big spiritual questions while simultaneously making a commitment to continue to be of service to the world. I remain determined to pursue joy, while advancing my capacity to embrace life as it comes. While there may, indeed, be many opportunities for paradox, there need not be a dichotomy. In the words of my friend, author Connie Goldman, we can aspire to not only grow old, but to grow whole.[2]

3

The Seeker's Guide

Navigating the Wild Space beyond Midlife

ASK AND YE SHALL RECEIVE:
QUESTIONS AS SPIRITUAL EXERCISE

Thousands of years ago a young mystic climbed the tallest mountain in the land. He was determined to sit in deep contemplation until he had the answer to the question: "What is the meaning of life?"

The mystic meditated on the mountaintop over the years and decades, growing into a very old man. Over the span of his life, his reputation for devotion and wisdom spread far and wide. At last, the rumor began circulating through the village below that the spiritual master would soon be reaching the end of his life.

A young seeker, exactly the same age as the mystic was when he made his pilgrimage to the mountaintop, determined to do whatever it would take to find this great teacher and ask him the answer to what had been the subject of his lifelong quest.

After hiking many days, he sat at his guru's feet, eager to ask his urgent question.

"Master, what is the meaning of life?" The guru turned his gaze away from the horizon and looked straight into the devotee's eyes.

"Ah, my child," he said at last. "I have pondered this for many years and at long last, I have the answer. It's the sunset."

"The sunset? That's it? That's the meaning of life?" the seeker replied.

There was a long pause. Then the guru replied: "You mean it's not the sunset?"[1]

Like the guru and the devotee, we would all dearly like to receive clear and definitive answers to our questions not only about the meaning of life, but all manner of ultimate concerns. But the fact is, in a universe in which paradox abounds, meaning so often eludes us, and a power greater than ourselves is so frequently shrouded in deep mystery, it is often only the questions themselves that are readily available to us, engaging our spirits and capable of advancing us down the spiritual path.

The Primacy of Questions

It is no wonder that asking questions plays a central role in spiritual practice in the majority of philosophical, religious, and spiritual traditions. From the Zen koan and Socratic dialogue to Ignatian discernment and Talmudic discourse, seekers from across millennia, geographies, and beliefs share this most basic spiritual impulse in common.

The word *question* derives from the Latin *quaerere,* which means "to seek" or "to ask," closely related to the Latin for *quest.* The quest in the spiritual sense stems from the common impulse to convert doubt, fear, and confusion as well as love, trust, and compassion, into words that have the capacity to serve as the vehicle for entrance into a deeper relationship with ourselves, others, and the Sacred. Often, we must content ourselves with the spiritual path as a process, finding strength, comfort, and hope in our faith that by the mere fact of questioning, we are being taken ever nearer to the answers we seek.

In John's Gospel, in the very first chapter, one of the disciples is asked a question, one of the first among many that plays a critical role in the Christian tradition. The essence of the exchange is this: Jesus asks "What are you looking for?" and the disciple asks in return, "Where are you staying?" To this Jesus replies "Come and see" (John 1:38–39). The teacher's purpose is to invite the questioner into the deeper possibilities of life.

One of the significant contributions of Ignatius of Loyola, founder of the Jesuits and author of the *Spiritual Exercises* (SE), is what he called "discernment."[2] The SE is a manual of exercises for spiritual growth based on Ignatius's own spiritual journey. Through his experience of prayer, meditation, and contemplation, he discovered that he had to question what is experienced as a result of these spiritual exercises. When it was time to make a decision, he stepped back, observed, and studied what he was experiencing in order to be clear about which decision he should embrace.

In the twelfth century the Jewish philosopher Maimonides acknowledged the primacy of inquiry with his classic work, *Guide to the Perplexed*.[3] In this seminal text he addressed such compelling questions as "How should we describe God?" and "If God created the universe, why is there evil?" Following the Talmudic method in Judaism, students are trained and encouraged to ask insightful questions of not only the original text but also the commentaries by scholars who have contributed to the dialogue over the centuries. In the Jewish tradition it is commonly understood that the purpose of this method is to take the Talmudist beneath the interpretations, always in search of the deeper principle underlying meaning. In seeking clarification and illumination, seekers utilize the question and response format in the quest for reconciliation of apparent contradictions.

Questions at Midlife and Beyond

As we enter the years at midlife and beyond, our questions take on added urgency. We encounter questions of meaning and purpose and the confrontation of mortality that we were able to deny in our youth, but can no longer put off or ignore. It is in the face of ultimate reality that our quest and our seeking can become even more pressing and relevant in our daily lives.

One of our contemporary influences, who shared the privileging of questions in a book each of us had discovered independently, is Jungian psychoanalyst James Hollis, author of *Finding Meaning in the Second Half of Life: How to Finally, Really Grow Up*. In the book the seminal question is posed: What does it really mean to be a grown-up in today's world? followed by a series of questions that address this core concern from different perspectives, alternately guiding and teasing us toward increased wisdom.[4]

No Small Order

Engaging with irresolution in service of increasing wisdom is no small order, as you face the questions that beg to be answered in life's second half. It is human nature to want the quick answer that will resolve all. More to the point, we all want whatever IT is, yesterday!

Against this tendency we would ask, instead, that you take

our guidance by joining with those from the many traditions whose spiritual leadership stems from being willing to ask questions and wait patiently for a response. In fact, the true spiritual leader remains passionately interested in the mystery, the inquiry, the question, understanding the limits to his or her knowledge. The fruits of such a spirituality include childlike wonder, astonishment, compassion, fascination, awe, and along with yet more questions, the invitation to go out and play.

LESSONS LEARNED

Spiritual counselors learn this lesson early in their training. When Carol sought postdoctoral certification in spiritual counseling at the New Seminary in Manhattan, the first lesson she learned was that providing guidance to clients was not about sharing her knowledge and advice. In fact, what was meant to transpire in the counseling relationship wasn't about her at all. Rather, it was the spiritual counselor's task to step out of the way in order to help facilitate a direct relationship between the seeker and the Divine.

Psychologists, just as surely as spiritual seekers, also have much to gain from this more humble approach to life. When Bob entered his career as a psychologist, his own anxiety necessitated that he know and understand both himself and his clients with absolute certainty. Not knowing was not an option. Over time, however, Bob came to a new understanding of his work. An encounter with one particular patient, who was ending her work with Bob after a long period of intensive psychotherapy, was a watershed moment.

In the last session Bob asked what had been most useful about their work together. She replied, "I can tell you this, Dr. Weber, it was not your brilliant interpretations! It was because you said you'd be here every week, and you were!" In that moment Bob experienced a profound sense of relief because he realized he did not have to be "brilliant," to have all the answers or interpretations, perfectly and flawlessly articulated, as he had imagined. Not knowing was an option! In fact, this was the only option, given the reality of the mystery of the person with whom he sat week in and week out. Most important was being present to one's self, in the moment, in the now. From that point on Bob no longer felt it his duty to lead the process of therapy. Rather he only needed to be able to follow his patient's process and work collaboratively. Therapist and client became two people, as mysterious to themselves as to one another, and that was all right. In fact, it was more than all right. It was the truth.

Carol had a similar breakthrough moment in her training as a spiritual counselor when she role-played an encounter with a client undergoing a personal crisis. Coming to this training from her background as a professor and author/speaker, Carol was used to being in the role of the one with answers, or at least informed opinions. But partway into this particular exercise, she realized that the fellow student playing the role of client was not just acting, but sharing something real, deep, and personal with her. Carol found herself uncharacteristically tongue-tied, staying as present as possible to her subject through the discomfort of not being able to conjure up a single helpful thing to say. At last, having struggled for long minutes with her desire to do something that would alleviate both her and her client's discomfort, she finally gave up and simply listened.

The exercise continued for a half hour more, her teacher and observers paying rapt attention. When, at last, the teacher called time, Carol was sure she had let both her client and the class down. Instead, she was astonished when her role-playing partner turned directly to her, tears streaming down his cheeks: "How can I ever thank you enough for what you said. It was just what I needed to hear." The truth is that Carol had remained silent through most of the session, and yet it had been her most effective encounter to date.

RELAX THE GRIP

The essence of what Bob and Carol learned is this: we cannot drive life, white knuckles on the wheel of destiny, heading toward what we have been led to believe in our American culture represents success and achievement. We keep making the effort only because we cannot bear the anxiety of letting go and confronting what becomes increasingly obvious to us as we age: that while we can influence much of what happens to us along the way, ultimately, it is not we who are calling the shots. Hopefully, by journeying with us through the questions in this book, you will find yourself enabled at last to relax your grip on the wheel of life. In its place you can increasingly relish the journey itself, as well as find yourself in unexpected places beyond your own imagining and effort.

This is the heart of what we are inviting our readers to do with us: to willingly enter the second half of life, the challenges and opportunities, and to face the hard questions that it raises; to not avoid the questions and to not settle for answers that are not true to the questions. Asking questions stirs us up, marching us to the edge of human knowledge and personal limitations. But paradoxically, surrendering to the questions—allowing them to move us along the spiritual path—provides the very means to embrace the experience of wholeness we want most.

PART II

(6)

25 QUESTIONS
*A Journey
of Spiritual Inquiry*

WE BEGIN THE BODY OF OUR BOOK with a series of questions that will guide you to take a deeper look not only at where you are coming from, but the progress you've made over time in the direction of what we call "spiritual maturity." Along the way the very act of engaging with these questions holds the potential to transform aging not only into a spiritual path, but into a mystical experience.

Building on thousands of years of tradition, we trust that both our questions and our commentary will contribute to your journey as you seek to live ever more fully, no matter what you are facing in your life, and the concerns and possibilities you entertain.

What Is Spiritual Maturity?

1. What is a psychologically and spiritually healthy vision of aging?

2. How has your spirituality changed and deepened over time?

3. How have your notions of the Divine matured since you were a child?

4. What is the relationship between spirituality and religion?

5. How can you assess your progress toward a more mature spirituality?

THE QUESTION OF SPIRITUAL MATURITY

How do we define spiritual maturity? Spiritual maturity is a stage in our development that allows us to look life in the eye, without denial, intensely appreciative and deeply trusting, even as we embrace the shadows and uncertainties. Theologians, philosophers, developmental psychologists, and even neurobiologists note that there are remarkable similarities ascribed to the peak of human development. Clearly there is a correlation between the devotion to spiritual practice over time and qualities we aspire to increasingly incorporate into our lives as we age: compassion, acceptance, peace, gratitude, forgiveness, and the like.

The implication of models of spiritual growth, however, is equally clear. Spiritual maturity is not something we attain once and for all. Rather, it is a process of lifelong evolution and development, beginning at birth and continuing until our final breath. Along the way we discover, time and again, that the spiritual path can be full of bumps and potholes. We stumble often, our vision clouded and blurred by the people, things, and events in our lives and the responses that arise within us. The good news is that whether we walk this path in a state of peace or of struggle, as long as we keep putting one foot ahead of the other, we are making progress.

Ironically, the further we travel from our early conceptions of the Sacred and meaning toward spiritual maturity, the more childlike we have the potential to become. But "like a child" is not the same as "childish." As we progress we have the potential to attain a newfound sense of wonder, an inner freedom we may not have experienced since early childhood. We may find ourselves with an increased attentiveness to the little things in nature, in others, and in ourselves, accompanied by a sense of awe. It is possible to experience this even as our aging bodies feel the weight of the years.

As we move through the second half of our lives, there will be times we will be perplexed by the questions our changing life circumstances will raise. At such times it will be important to have laid a strong foundation upon which to build. Engaging deeply with the questions in this book is a great beginning, but we are all still works in progress. Expect that you will be called to ask yourself many more questions over the course of your life to come, seeking answers that open your eyes to newly presenting spiritual opportunities as they continue to unfold.

Like Paul, who was knocked off his high horse on the road to Damascus and blinded by a bright light, we will need to journey to a place where we can get what we need to recover our sight (Acts 9:3–4). These questions point the way.

Question 1
What is a psychologically and spiritually healthy vision of aging?
Carol Orsborn

In the first chapter Bob and I identify what is most problematic about the dominant popular and academic notions of aging that hold sway in society today. In a nutshell it is the failure to recognize the growth opportunity in growing older, which takes into consideration both the shadow and the light. In skewing the picture toward extremes of positives and negatives, what is left out is a psychologically and spiritually healthy vision of aging that is grounded both in reality and hope.

What do we mean by this? Here is a simple assessment you

can administer to yourself to ascertain what theories of aging have been operative in your life. To begin I ask you to imagine an elderly woman on a park bench staring vacantly into space. What do you assume about her? If your knee-jerk reaction is that she is depressed and marginalized, and that this is a problem, you have been influenced by activity theory. If you believe she is fading away from life, a kind of graceful receding into death, but that this is okay, you have been influenced by disengagement theory. If you resist doing this exercise at all, you may be in denial. But if you are even willing to entertain the notion that she is having a transcendent experience, not disengaged or marginalized by life, but rather, embracing the whole of it in a state of ecstatic, unspoken awe, you are a gerontological pioneer, on the forefront of identifying a radically new and exciting vision of aging and a new understanding of the opportunities aging can present to us.

This notion of aging goes beyond seeing spirituality as a component to making the most out of aging by mitigating the negative effects as much as possible. Rather, this new approach actually perceives aging as a spiritual path, in and of itself. This includes even what is conventionally described as the negative aspects of aging, such as diminishment of ego, increasing losses, even pain and suffering, as serving in the capacity of advancement of spiritual maturity. The cohort that is most closely aligned with this new understanding of the opportunities of aging is the conscious aging movement referenced earlier, although as both Bob and I reveal, there are elements, lessons, and approaches to making the shift from aging as problem to aging as spiritual path to be found in virtually every religious and spiritual tradition.

For me, personally, this represents a tectonic shift in understanding. Just four years ago, when I turned sixty-three, I plummeted headfirst from romanticized notions of aging into dread and fear, a descent (and redemption) I chronicled in my memoir *Fierce with Age: Chasing God and Squirrels in Brooklyn.* Over the course of that year, dealing with the unwanted physical, social, and emotional ramifications of growing older, I was forced to face my inability to make things turn out the way I wanted. I was initially shocked, then increasingly humbled, to discover that so many of my old tricks were no longer working. But along the way, I also ironically began to realize how much of what I'd experienced as a sense of mastery had been mostly smoke and mirrors in the first place. At last I was forced to let go of the illusion that it was I who had been calling the shots and to confront the truth of my limitations.

As I captured in one of my journal entries toward the end of that year:

> As it turns out, when viewed through the lens of psychological and spiritual maturity, this is a good thing. When we strip away the impositions, the fantasies, and the denial, we begin to view aging as holding the potential for activation of new, unprecedented levels of self-affirmation, meaning, and spiritual growth.

As I have discovered, this psychologically and spiritually healthy vision of aging leaves space for peace and serenity. But it also allows for the possibility of making trouble, upsetting apple carts, and living life as fully as possible.

For me a psychologically and spiritually healthy vision of aging now includes the freedom and courage to expand my capacity to give and receive love, and to do whatever I can, sometimes big, sometimes small, to make a difference to others. As long as I keep growing, there will be anxious moments, regrets, and self-doubt. But there will be transiting, transforming, and overcoming, too. [1]

Paradoxically, I have come to discover that the more I surrender the illusion of control, the less I worry about what others think of me and the greater level of inner freedom I experience. Untangling from society's web, I envision old age as a time for creativity for its own sake, no longer needing to commoditize my talents and skills. That woman on the bench: maybe she is depressed. Maybe she's marginalized. But maybe she's me, just resting before she finishes her brisk walk, trying to come up with a title for her next book, or simply enjoying the moment.

I aspire to have many opportunities to ask myself a seminal question, framed so pointedly by psychologist and mystic Jim Finley: "What would become of me if I were to surrender completely to this grace?"[2] In the very act of asking this question of myself, I have turned the corner from resistance to the fearful stereotypes of aging to instead plunge into the very heart of growing older.

What is a psychologically and spiritually healthy vision of aging?

Bob Weber

For a number of years, I had been noticing a gradual loss of clear-sightedness. Despite the fact that my ophthalmologist had diagnosed the presence of cataracts, I seemed to be, at best, semiconscious of what was actually happening. Now, as I look back on this period, I believe that this was due to a "denial" of my getting older. Only older folks need such a surgical procedure!

Finally, in the fall of 2011, surgery was warranted since the cataracts had "ripened" sufficiently. After we set the dates for the surgery, the reality, both of the cataracts and of my aging, could no longer be denied. This awakening was verified the following June of 2011, when I received my Medicare card, and my wife said, half-jokingly, that I was becoming "an old man."

While I had some misgiving about this fact, I actually found myself appreciating and even enjoying this evolution, just as I enjoyed the outcome of my surgery. Vividly, I recall the new experience of my own eyesight. I could not remember ever seeing so clearly, appreciating colors so powerfully, and no longer being subject to the glare of lights at night that created danger when I drove. I could see more clearly in the "daylight" and drive more confidently through the "dark night."

As time goes on I am realizing how alike psychological and spiritual maturity are in many respects. As a psychologist involved in the professional practice of psychotherapy, I could see that what I hoped for my patients was not unlike what I desired for myself in my personal spiritual practice.

One of the first goals of psychoanalytic psychotherapy is to move from a sleepy state of unconsciousness to a state of greater consciousness about what I think, how I feel, and what I do, so I can live life more fully and freely. A second goal of therapy is to correct the many distortions that are fostered by the unconscious state of life—distortions about myself, about others, and about life in general. The third goal is to move to a greater freedom, to be the subject, the active agent of our lives. Fourth, as we work through the preceding goals, we slowly but surely develop a deeper sense of our own worth and value as a human being.

This sense of the congruence between psychology and spirituality was reinforced when I began to read the works of Anthony de Mello, a psychotherapist, an Indian Jesuit, and a spiritual director and priest. In his book *Walking on Water,* he wrote that spirituality is: (1) awakening; (2) living without illusions; (3) never being at the mercy of any person, thing, or event; and (4) discovering and appreciating the diamond mine inside yourself.[3] His conceptualization of spirituality is resonant with the psychoanalytic paradigm, but for de Mello and me, this is a conception that includes one other essential element, which Sigmund Freud did not include—God.

In a book titled *The Psychology of Mature Spirituality,* authors Polly Young-Eisendrath and Melvin E. Miller characterize mature spirituality as having three dimensions: integrity, wisdom, and transcendence.[4] As defined earlier, ego integrity and wisdom are the terms Erik Erikson used to discuss the final developmental stage of life, old age.[5] Living into this stage gives us the opportunity to integrate all the pieces of our lives: the good, the bad, and the ugly. If this goes undone, or is incompletely done, despair occurs. The fruit of this integration is wisdom, seeing the truth of life more clearly because we have lived and are living it freely and fully.

This results in a transcendent perspective, not because we have bypassed the concrete and finite reality of our lives, but because we have entered it and experienced it more deeply, with a vision that even enables us to see into and through what Rabbi Irwin Kula, in his book, *Yearnings,* calls "the sacred messiness of life."[6]

Question 2

How has your spirituality changed and deepened over time?

Bob Weber

A Portuguese proverb says, "God writes straight with crooked lines." My life is testimony to the truth of this. When I was younger, I believed that life in general and my own life in particular were linear. I was so sure of myself. One certainty was that I would one day become a priest. My father even predicted that I would one day be ordained. His dream for me became my dream as well. How could I not wish to please my father, the person whom I loved deeply and passionately!

Although he wanted me to become a priest, he discouraged me from entering a seminary at too early an age, despite my parish priest's encouragement to enter a high school prep seminary. My father "predicted" that I would go to high school, succeed at academics and athletics, and do the same in college. After all this prophecy was fulfilled, then I would prepare for the priesthood.

That day finally arrived while I was in my first year of graduate school, preparing for a career in education. A series of events and people conspired and led me to enter the Jesuit community and begin the road to priesthood. At the time of my decision, I was never so sure of anything I had ever done. I was sure I was living what I had read about "vocation" in Thomas Merton's *No Man Is an Island:* "Every man has a vocation to be someone: but he must understand clearly that in order to fulfill his vocation he can only be one person: himself."[7] I had arrived—or, so I thought.

After many fruitful and growth-producing years as a Jesuit, I became depressed, yet continued to live my vowed life. At last I took a leave of absence to sort out my doubts and confusion. With the guidance and encouragement of very good spiritual directors, I finally made the decision to leave the Jesuit community, with considerable sadness and certainty.

Gradually, the peace that ensued confirmed my decision, despite my father's initial reaction of anger and upset at me for changing my mind and disappointing his dreams. Eventually, he was able to say that all he ever wanted for me was my happiness. Even if he had never been able to say this, I knew that the decision was my truth.

In time I married and completed my doctoral degree in clinical psychology. Now I have been working as a psychologist for nearly forty years. All the crooked lines are converging at an intersection as I work to integrate three major threads of my life: my profession as a psychologist, my own aging and interest in gerontology, and my lifelong commitment to living a spiritual life. All three and their interweaving provide service to others. God does indeed "write straight with crooked lines."

How has your spirituality changed and deepened over time?
Carol Orsborn

In many premodern cultures, there is a classic coming-of-age ritual in which the adolescent is separated from the familiarity of the everyday life of the tribe. Whether he or she is left alone in the wilderness, isolated in a hut, or tied to a tree to be bitten by red ants, the heart of the ordeal is the same. To grow into adulthood, the youth must endure a series of trials that initiate the participant into a new life stage.

Social scientists suggest that individuals undergoing transition at any stage of their lives go through a similar transformative sequence, often resulting in spiritual growth. One particularly useful model for lifelong growth is Drs. David Feinstein and Stanley Krippners' work on cultural mythology.[8] I was introduced to this work by my coresearcher Dr. Jimmy Laura Smull, with whom I coauthored the book *The Silver Pearl: Our Generation's Journey to Wisdom*. According to this model the child is born into an original worldview—including religious and spiritual beliefs. It is these beliefs, constructions, and understandings about how the world works that give the child's life meaning. In healthy development, when the individual encounters new information that differs from the original "myth," the maturing individual either modifies or replaces it. In effect, one becomes literally dis-illusioned of one's original programming, only to make space for new, more authentic understandings to take their place. The stakes of disillusionment are high, however, as in many formulations, we are taught that if we disagree with the authorities who have told us what to believe, it is we who are wrong, crazy, bad, or doomed. And yet, many of us reach a point where we are no longer willing to deny our own sense of life, meaning, and truth.

For many of us initiation into a more mature spirituality is a lifelong and recurring process. There are many catalysts that force us to go deeper, not only external triggers such as illness, divorce, financial issues, or moving away from home. But also, such internal instigators as the inability to make a decision, the nagging sense that you are perceived by others differently than how you feel inside, persistent self-neglect of your physical or emotional needs, free-floating anxiety, and the like. At last, you confront these messages head-on, not as problems to be solved, but as opportunities for growth. For at the same time old conceptions are passing away, signs of new behavior, attitudes, and beliefs are sending up sprouts.

At first the tendency is to rebel against the illusions of your youth. Whatever notions you were taught as a child, you are likely to feel inspired to do exactly the opposite. In doing so you may well believe that at last you have found freedom, but the truth is that as long as you are driven by knee-jerk reactivity to the past, you have only replaced one set of programming with another set of likewise limiting beliefs. But don't despair. In the words of Bill Bridges, who wrote about disillusionment in his book, *Transitions:* "One must surrender and give into the emptiness and stop struggling to escape it. Chaos is not a mess. Rather it is the primal state of pure energy to which the person returns for every true new beginning. It is only from the perspective of the old form that chaos looks fearful. From any other perspective, it looks like life itself, as yet unshaped by purpose and identification."9

While disillusionment is not something we would ever wish upon ourselves, it does herald a new period of spiritual growth. Eventually we move beyond both passive victimization and reactive rebelliousness to become what some psychological formulations and spiritual traditions refer to as "actualized." The hallmark of actualization is authenticity: becoming a whole that is capable of embracing opposing tensions. Mature spirituality is unshakable, specifically because it includes everything, leaving nothing out. Of course we yearn for serenity, to feel resolved and secure about the future, and to experience profound joy, fresh and appropriate in the present moment. We relish those moments when—as the mystics describe it—"heaven reaches down and kisses the earth." But as we become actualized, we come to realize that the sublime is only part of the whole picture. Having worked so hard to reclaim a worldview that offers the promise of mature spirituality, we are more likely to reach exalted states on a more consistent basis.

But, as my coresearcher Jimmy Smull and I, and the hundreds of women fifty plus who participated in our study, came to understand, what catches us by surprise is that even when we are in pain—at those difficult times when we find ourselves struggling with grief, anxiety, anger, or any of the other darker tones on the emotional scale—we still think the spiritual path we're on is a journey well worth taking.

Question 3
How have your notions of the Divine matured since you were a child?
Carol Orsborn

When I was very young, my parents took me to visit Santa Claus. I remember vividly the department store, full of bright green holly and red poinsettias. We stood in line, and the longer we waited, the more apprehensive I became. No amount of jingling bells and colorful balloons could touch the gathering anxiety. When at last I was placed on Santa's lap, my nervous stomach erupted and I threw up on Jolly Old St. Nick. He wasn't pleased.

In the Jewish tradition, we believe that it is beyond human capacity to portray, visualize, or even refer to God by name. So, for me, the secularized Santa sitting in a department store was about as close as I could get to imagining my relationship to the Divine. More to the point this Santa's unfortunate response was proof of what I'd always suspected: there is a power greater than ourselves, beguiling on the surface, but quick to shame.

Perhaps you won't find it a stretch of the imagination that I became a perfectionist. I really wanted to be good. But much like Pooh Bear stuck in the honey pot, I seemed always to be in one sort of trouble or another. In my tradition there was no talk of the raging fires of hell. But the chief rabbi of my congregation made it very clear: God could only tolerate my stretching the tradition so far. In fact, I was twenty-one before I discovered exactly where the boundary was to be found. I had fallen in love with a Christian. In those days interfaith marriages were a rarity—beyond the pale of even our liberal temple. So when we asked our rabbi to marry us, he said no.

Having gone off to college four years prior, I'd been exposed to many other traditions, beliefs, and conceptions of God. While I took this rejection as a blow, I did not turn away from spirituality and religion. In fact, it catapulted me forward into a new conception of God.

To make a long story short, I stopped worrying about pleasing a judgmental God, replacing this with a new, but not necessarily improved, strategy: I started giving God orders. Exploring everything from positive thinking to the martial arts and the consciousness movement, I routinely wrote out affirmations that custom-ordered the results I expected to receive, when and where I wanted them. In retrospect I realize how compassionate and loving it was that God met my impudence and hubris with such patience.

My confidence that God was my special assistant began eroding long before I had a life-changing crisis: a diagnosis of breast cancer in 1997. Facing mortality has a way of quickening the learning curve. In fact, there's a great story from the Twelve Step Tradition that describes exactly where I was at.

A young woman is taking a walk along a mountain path when she slips and falls. She grabs onto a branch and is hanging precipitously over a thousand feet abyss. Now, this woman always believed in God, but had taken the relationship for granted. Suddenly, the thought occurred to her that this would be a good time to reach out to God and ask for help.

"God, are you up there?" she cried out.

"Yes, my child. I'm here. What do you need?"

"God, I'm terrified, hanging here over the cliff. What should I do?" Just then the branch began to crack. "God, I beg you tell me. I'll do whatever you ask."

God replied, "Let go of the branch."

"Let go of the branch?"

"Yes, my child. Let go of the branch."

There was a long pause. She looked down. She looked up again. At last, the girl cried out: "Is there anybody else up there?"

As a result of my brush with mortality, I was graced with a much deeper and more profound understanding of God. It was never God's job to deliver to me what I want in reward for obedience or in recognition of my special charms. Rather, God is the one who is asking me to trust enough to let go.

How have your notions of the Divine matured since you were a child?

Bob Weber

In 1979 Ana-Marie Rizzuto, M.D., a psychoanalyst in Boston, published *The Birth of the Living God: A Psychoanalytic Study.* In her book she examined the images of God that four people developed over time and the basis for the different visions of

God that emerged for them. These case studies provided four different pictures of God—a God "without whiskers," a God "in the mirror," God, "the enigma," and God, "my enemy."[10]

Not long before Rizzuto's book appeared, I had been struggling with my own image of God during my discernment about my Jesuit vocation. Discernment is a prayerful, spiritually directed, decision-making process, which in this instance led me to leave the Jesuit community I had joined ten years earlier. At one juncture in my prayer, an image of God appeared and a turning point occurred.

What I recall about that moment was a God who was harsh, judgmental, and punitive, a God more inclined to condemn than mercifully forgive, a God more given to wrath than to love. In that moment anger welled up inside me. I raised my fist, looked to heaven, and said with a rage that was embellished by a few four-letter words, "If this is the kind of God you are, get lost, I want nothing to do with you!"

Then, a fear overtook me, and I imagined the sky opening and the wrath of God pouring out over me and reducing me to nothing. Instead I experienced a peaceful silence, deeper than I had ever known. I breathed a sigh of relief. A sense of God's mercy, forgiveness, and love arose and persisted over the years as I pressed on with my life. Although there has been an occasional, residual dread of condemnation, it predominated no longer.

My experience resembled that of Elijah the prophet. When Elijah fled to Mount Horeb in order to avoid the murderous wrath of the prophets of Ba'al, he was consoled after God revealed himself, not in the storm or howling wind, but in the stillness.

Now there was a great wind, so strong that it was splitting mountains and breaking rocks in pieces before the Lord, but

the Lord was not in the wind; and after the wind an earth-
quake, but the Lord was not in the earthquake; and after the
earthquake a fire, but the Lord was not in the fire; and after
the fire a sound of sheer silence. (1 Kings 19:11)

Like Elijah what I experienced was the God I had known as
a child, when I would attend the 6:30 a.m. Mass at my parish, in
the quiet of dawn's half-light. There was a peaceful stillness, without any particular image of God. Now I would say it was God the
Father, an image of God derived from my relationship with my
own father whom I deeply loved and admired as a young child.

Over time this image was tainted by the influence of the
teaching of a pre–Vatican II Roman Catholic Church that
stressed sin and confession and enlarged my own harsh super-
ego. Weekly, sometimes daily, if I thought I had committed a
mortal sin, I would take my scrupulous, superego-plagued self
to confession. Fortunately, only once in all my confessing years
did I experience a priest who made me feel even more guilty and
hopeless after confession.

As I confessed my sins, that one priest kept asking questions
such as, "Are you sure you didn't do that more times than you
just said? What other sins have you not yet mentioned?" Slowly,
I realized he was communicating a sense that I was condemned,
not redeemed. He was missing the whole point of the confessional experience.

My fist-raising moment purged me of whatever vestiges of
this priest and the punishing, condemning God he represented
still remained within me. It also freed me of the punitive super-
ego and its accompanying scrupulosity with which I conducted
my life. Finally, I was free, to live.

While a Jesuit I discovered strong parallels between my

experience and that of Ignatius of Loyola, founder of the community known as the Society of Jesus. He had also struggled with scrupulosity during a period of his spiritual journey that was laden with a heightened sensitivity to his capacity for sin. It took a confessor saying to him, essentially, "Stop it! and get on with your life." When Ignatius wrote his *Spiritual Exercises* he included a lengthy section dealing with rules to manage scrupulosity.[11]

Question 4
What is the relationship between spirituality and religion?
Bob Weber

Harvey Cox, a well-known Harvard Divinity School theologian, speaks about a cohort of people that have emerged on the American religious-cultural landscape, "SBNR's." An SBNR is someone who is "spiritual, but not religious."[12] This group is largely, though not exclusively, composed of the baby boomer generation, Carol's and my generation, born during the post–World War II period that produced economic prosperity and large population growth as soldiers returned home and settled back into domestic and family life.

In his sociological studies of this boomer generation, Wade Clark Roof called attention to the conditions in American culture that contributed to what made us tick in the religious and spiritual realm(s). *A Generation of Seekers: The Spiritual Journeys of the Baby Boom Generation,* according to a New York Times book review, charted "the currents of belief for the generation that rebelled" and concluded that "the outsized generation born between 1946 and 1964 is now turning to religion. This is the group that was spiritually shaken by the 1960s, felt the after-shocks of the 1970s, and by their numbers alone, became a bat-tering ram for social change." In essence this tumultuous process has been a "search for meaning and values in a complex world" that still continues.[13]

Several years later Roof returned to interview many of those who were the basis for his original study. He wrote a second book, *Spiritual Marketplace: Baby Boomers and the Remaking of American Religion,* and concluded that a shift was occurring "away from religion as traditionally understood to more diverse and creative approaches." He observed that this religious diver-sity was reflected in the kind of books being stocked under "Religion" at the chain book stores, books on a wide variety of religious and spiritual topics, for example, "angels, Sufism, journey, recovery, meditation, magic, inspiration, Judaica, astrol-ogy, gurus, Bible, prophecy, evangelicalism, Mary, Buddhism, Catholicism, and esoterica."[14] I continue to witness this change, thirteen years after his book's publication, in the bookstores of Harvard Square.

Roof identified five emergent subcultures in the "spiritual marketplace": dogmatists, born-again Christians, mainstream believers, metaphysical believers and seekers, and secularists, organizing them around their contrasting religious and spiri-tual identities.[15] Of course, I had to place myself in one of the categories or conceptualize an entirely new one. First, I elimi-nated those I knew I was not, leaving one category, "mainstream believer." As such, in Roof's typology, I am one who is "religious and spiritual," not the more fashionable SBNR.

Many of my professional colleagues and even a number of my personal friends cannot understand why I remain a Catholic. They cannot comprehend how an educated person continues to adhere to a religion that seems to require childish submission to an institution, the Church, that professes belief in a story that seems like a fairy tale, that practices rituals that seem ridiculous to them, and that offers a community of people often so different than I.

That is the nature of religion. Put in its simplest terms, it is a community of belief, accompanied by rituals and practices that manifest, support, and deepen the beliefs. It does sound a bit like child's play! However, it is anything but, for its life blood is the spiritual life it is intended to cultivate and nurture, a way of life and being that far surpasses the more culturally acceptable images of maturity—success and status, prestige and wealth.

The spiritual life as I experience it awakens me to what really counts and helps me see what really matters. It helps me penetrate the falseness that pervades much of life and dispels the illusions that we as individuals and cultures create for ourselves. George Carlin said it well, "They call it the American dream because you have to be asleep to believe it."[16] A deepening spirituality also frees me from being at the mercy of any person, thing, or event, putting everything in proper perspective. And this spiritual life enables me to bear my dignity as a human being, beloved and blessed, even if it is difficult to see it in the midst of more difficult times.

For many people mainstream religion no longer works. In discussing spirituality and religion, the Jesuit priest Anthony de Mello describes that nature of spirituality, adding that "religion is intended to lead you there."[17] For many in Roof's studies, the metaphysical believers and seekers and the secularists, traditional religion no longer serves that purpose. My Roman Catholic background still serves my spiritual quest, although it has become nuanced over the years. Many, including my wife, cannot understand how I can abide it, given its many problems and scandals, particularly the sexual abuses by priests and the slow regression and retrenchment in a pre–Vatican II culture.

My answer is simple. My spirituality and faith sustain me through all the complexities of life. The God in whom I place my faith is merciful and forgiving, slow to anger, abounding in kindness and compassion (so much so that he joined us through the incarnation), and who is, above all else, loving; he considers me—yes, all of us—beloved even when I am prodigal.

These days I am further bolstered by the advent of the Church's new leader, Pope Francis, who is helping us envision a church that places greater emphasis on pastoral flexibility than on dogmatic rigidity.

What is the relationship between spirituality and religion?
Carol Orsborn

Your whole life is enmeshed in great and living forces: terrible because unknown.
EVELYN UNDERHILL

I begin addressing the distinction between religion and spirituality with an irony: at their best, there is no difference. Spirituality is essentially an intimately personal and direct relationship to a power greater than one's ordinary self. At the core of every major religious tradition there is a progenitor: someone who not only experienced this unity personally, but was able to articulate and transmit the power of the Divine to others. Be it Moses and Abraham giving birth to Judaism, Jesus for Christianity, Mohammed for Islam, or Buddha for Buddhism, in the beginning, spirituality and religion were merged.

When spirituality grows beyond individual experience and into community, however, there are challenges. As the generations succeed one another, the tendency is for the original spiritual core to solidify into doctrine, for the direct experience of the Divine to be ordered into rules and codes by interpreters.

When religion puts form and obedience ahead of spiritual truth, it becomes easier—in fact, more expedient—for the communal leadership to make promises that can't be kept. "Just do as we say and nothing bad will happen to you. If you do stray, you will be punished." Individuals who resist such manipulations are accused of disloyalty, cast aside or down. But always, there is the potential for the Divine to break through, regardless of whether one is in a healthy religious institution or not. God can find us wherever we are, in our pain, in our dysfunctions, as well as in our joy and breakthroughs.

But sometimes, hopefully frequently, religion rises above the tendencies to distance and solidify, by offering the best of all worlds: both the respect and nurturing of the individual's direct relationship to the Divine, and the loving support, companionship, and guidance of a community of teachers and peers. You can palpably sense when a religious group is alive with spirit. The members of such a fortunate convergence experience themselves both as individuals and as a community, supported rather than undermined in the growing capacity to pay heed to the deepest yearnings of their souls.

It can take courage to break out of comfortable routines to breathe true life into one's relationship with the Divine. Facing a life-threatening illness, I was forced to confront my limitations, grappling with circumstances beyond my control. In the journal I was keeping at the time, I wrote that I believed I had found the outer boundary of my faith, tumbling over it headfirst into the void. But even while I was stripped bare by the events of my life as they unfolded, I had unwittingly turned myself into a candidate for intimacy with God, beyond anything I'd ever experienced before. Whether inside or outside a particular religious body or institution, life has a way of peeling back our false understandings of life, God, and meaning, down to the depths of mystery. In the darkness, I found myself stripped of my fondest notions, my comfort, and even the trust I had been putting into my spiritual practices. What then? I had to let go, finding it in myself to be able to wait, sometimes patiently, sometimes anxiously, whether alone or alongside others, for inspiration, meaning, and hope.

For those of us who aspire to living a mature spiritual life, the sacred duty is not to play a dutiful role to a religious community, but to open the windows so that the sounds of the wild can penetrate our heart with their music of awe and wonder.

As we live and breathe truth in the shadow of the mystery, neither true religion nor spirituality can guarantee outcomes, comfort, or security during the span of our life. What we get, however, is infinitely more. As J. MacMurray writes: "Fear not: The things that you are afraid of are quite likely to happen to you, but they are nothing to be afraid of."[18]

Question 5

How can you assess your progress toward a more mature spirituality?

Carol Orsborn

When I am face to face with audiences, I often ask: "Who knows more than they did ten years ago?" Invariably, every hand is raised. We do grow in many ways over time, including our level of spiritual maturity. But we cannot always measure our progress apart from how we approach the everyday challenges and opportunities with which we are faced. For example, how do you deal with setbacks in regard to your health? How is your relationship with your adult child? Have you made progress in regard to unfinished business, including both regrets and unfulfilled goals?

Previously, I referred to a research study I undertook in conjunction with social scientist Dr. Jimmy Laura Smull, in which we set out to observe how women, in particular, grow spiritually through the life stages at midlife and beyond. We gathered focus groups, did one-on-one and group interviews, and sent out surveys in search of mature women who had achieved mastery in one or more areas of their lives. The responses confirmed our theory: that unlike physical development, the older you become, the more possible it is for you to achieve your fullest psycho-spiritual potential.[19]

We didn't find many who had achieved mastery across the board. But many of us have areas in which we've progressed, and areas where we've stalled. Happily, spiritual as well as psychological growth can occur at any age. In fact, we discovered that discontent is one of the key indicators that you are progressing toward spiritual maturity: still striving, working toward and aiming for the fulfillment of life's promise.

We advance spiritually by leaving behind old beliefs and patterns that no longer serve us and acquiring new depths of awareness about who we are becoming. This is the entryway to spiritual growth—you must be willing to turn toward rather than away from the uncomfortable and unresolved issues in your life.

How can you assess your progress toward a more mature spirituality?

Bob Weber

How can you assess your progress toward a more mature spirituality? If you can understand this paradox: "unless you change and become like little children, you will never enter the Kingdom of Heaven" (Matthew 18:3).

You may have to turn your idea of mature spirituality on its head and, paradoxically, become childlike to be spiritually mature. Adults have many answers to many questions, even if they only pretend to know the answers sometimes. But doesn't being an expert who is mature spiritually suggest you have the answers? No, it means you are able to say "I don't know." At that point the "leap of faith" is possible.

Growing up I remember looking down on "doubting" Thomas whenever I heard his story. After the resurrection he was the "doubter," the one who said "unless"—"Unless I see the mark of the nails in his hands, and put my finger in the mark of the nails and my hand in his side, I will not believe" (John 20:25). However, this doubter who was plagued by questions and uncertainties eventually gave the most powerful profession of faith of them all: "My Lord and my God!" (John 20:28).

Of course, growing up as Catholic children, we were supposed to have the answers, answers ingrained in us through the Baltimore Catechism in anticipation of First Communion. More answers were drilled into us in preparation for confirmation, when the bishop who presided would spend time asking questions of the confirmation class and applauding the responses delivered with rote precision.

What did we really know at the time? Very little, if anything, given our short life spans and little life experience. How many of us sat there with real questions on our minds about life and faith? Now, with much more lived experience, more doubts have surfaced, more questions have emerged, and, probably, anxiety and fear have been cultivated as we have come to know how little we really know and how very little control we have over this mysterious life.

At last we have the chance to become experts at life. The potential has always been there; however, it has been obscured by our need to know, even when we did not. Perhaps this is the heart of the story of the Fall in the Old Testament Book of Genesis.

Remember the story: Adam and Eve were given free rein in Eden. They could taste the fruit from all the trees except that of the Tree of the Knowledge of Good and Evil. Before doing so they were like kids in a playground, enjoying everything around them, unself-conscious and filled with joy and, surely, awe before the mystery of it all. In the face of life's mysteries, kids ask questions, so much so that they drive their parents crazy at times with the barrage of "Whys?": Why is the sky blue? Why is there air? Why? Why? Why? As we become adults we no longer want the questions; we only want the answers. We become jaded and lose our capacity for wonder.

The French expression for "I wonder" is *Je me demande,* that is "I ask myself." To wonder is to be filled with questions, the way a child is who sees the world through fresh eyes. Only over time does this child in each of us develop "spiritual cataracts" that cloud our ability to experience true awe. It becomes so watered down in common parlance that its sacred sense is lost when co-opted by the culture to sustain and enhance illusions about life and worth. We have strayed from the real meaning of awe. How often we hear the expression "awesome." Has this jaded your appreciation of what awe really means?

Awe is a reverent wonder tinged with fear inspired by the sublime. If the words *fear* and *fearful* repulse you and dissuade you from wanting to experience true awe, let me tell you they repulsed me, too, initially. When I recall how much my early experience of religion and spirituality was laden with fear and dread, resulting in profound guilt and shame, my stomach turns into knots. This restricted my freedom to choose and kept me from becoming who I am today, a man living life vivaciously. After I discovered the real meaning of awe-related fear, freedom returned, as did fullness of life. So it is worth taking time to consider the true meaning contained in these words—awe is a reverent wonder tinged with fear inspired by the sublime— especially the word *sublime.*

In his article, "The repression of the sublime," Frank Haronian wrote, "it is out of a sense of boredom and dissatisfaction with the gratification of the senses that we begin to look for higher meanings in our life," and yearn for the sublime.[20] One dimension of this desire is "the need to ask and answer for oneself the basic existential question—Who am I? Where am I going?"[21] The fruit of this is experiencing the sublime: that which is most childlike, untainted by the jadedness of a socio-culturally reinforced persona of adulthood. In those sublime moments we have "the feeling of communion with and dedication to something that is greater than ourselves [and] we are experiencing this basic spiritual impulse. It may be religious, agnostic, or atheistic; it does not require belief in a God, but it is consonant with such a belief."[22]

This is an indicator of progress toward a mature spirituality! You will have become a child and entered the heavenly, spiritual realm.

5

What Is Spiritual Awakening?

6. Why do we want to stay asleep?

7. What wakes you up?

8. Has there been a particular experience that has finally awakened you?

9. What do you think the Sacred wants to awaken you to?

10. Is there a constructive role for regret, shame, and guilt?

THE QUESTION OF WAKING UP

Awakening! In the morning it is often difficult to rouse ourselves from sleep. Each morning provides various reasons to hit the snooze button and pull the covers up over our heads, sinking back into a state of sleepy unawareness, even when we realize it is "Time to get up!" Even during the day we often sleepwalk through our lives, going through the motions halfheartedly, semiconsciously, on autopilot.

In psychotherapy, too, people struggle to become more conscious of what is really going on internally. They remain mired in that which, if known, would free them from the very things about which they complain. People prefer the familiar and predictable even at the cost of a free and full life. In fact, people's purported problems are solutions that they are reluctant to give up. We see this in prison systems where inmates who are set free have a high rate of recidivism. And it is we ourselves who build the prisons in which we have incarcerated ourselves and serve death sentences.

The illusion is that we are safer by remaining so. As one man said, "I spent a lifetime building a fortress, only to discover that I actually created a prison for myself."[1] And in our self-made prisons, we squander our lives to avoid risks and fears associated with what we do not want to know.

It is not just we ourselves who create this state of affairs through our denial. We get plenty of help from our families, our institutions, and our culture, as the Buddha did before he woke up, experienced the reality of life and death, and made his way on the path to enlightenment. Buddha's father created a sheltered isolation to protect him from life's harsh realities. When, at last, Buddha went out into the streets of life, he shed the denial that he and his father had co-created, and he confronted for the first time, at twenty-nine, what had always been there—sickness, suffering, and death.

Ultimately, it is "the denial of death" that comes to the fore in the face of aging. As we noted previously a strong "antiaging culture" permeates our American society and has birthed a plethora of treatments and ointments and programs that support avoidance of aging by massive denial. But there is no escaping reality, especially in light of our generation's prospects for increased longevity. We may not want to "go gentle into that good night"[2]; however, one way or another, we have no choice but to go. The good news is that once we enter and set aside denial, we will discover a "dark night" that is paradoxically abundant in spiritual riches.

It is only when we bring ourselves, or we are brought, to face these fears that we awaken, get a breath of fresh air, and are able to LIVE—perhaps for the first time. As William Faulkner put it, "Be scared, you can't help that. But don't be afraid."[3]

Question 6
Why do we want to stay asleep?
Bob Weber

Do you put one too many pieces of chocolate candy in your mouth, throw down a few too many salty cashews without even thinking about it, or gulp more red wine from a glass without noticing it is your third glass? This is mindless eating.

It is also denial: denial about your already dangerously high cholesterol; denial about the added pounds that increase the risk to your health; and denial about the danger you face when driving home after the party. Yet at such times we move through the moments unconsciously, sleepwalking through the experience.

Why do we want to stay asleep, to remain in denial? Perhaps "want" is the wrong word. If it were just a matter of consciousness and we were fully aware of the cost to ourselves of remaining so, we would not continue to deny. Denial emerges from the very depths of our being, from those dimensions of our life that remain unconscious for the most part, for most of the time. These regions are the 80 percent of an iceberg that are not visible, that remain hidden beneath the surface, yet are nonetheless very much there.

Out of these depths comes the truth. We know that we are not really living our lives. Oh, yes, we think we are because we have acquired that which is admired by others, because we have a position of status and prestige in our world, and because everybody knows our name and speaks well of us. However, the deepest, the truest part of us does not navigate the world that bases value on what we have, what we do, and what others think of us. This part knows we are living a lie.

We are not responding to our vocation, to our call, to that voice deep within. First and foremost this vocation entails fully becoming the "human being" we are, through our choices, our decisions. The problem is that remaining asleep and in denial keeps us "human doings." It is only when the "being" and "doing" part of us are happily married that we become our true selves.

Opportunities for this reengagement with life, this coming alive in new ways, abound in midlife and beyond. And this requires facing all the risks involved, just as falling in love with someone is a very wonderful, frightening experience, especially when we consider the marital vows. We enter this relationship as we must enter life itself "for better or worse, for richer or poorer, in sickness and in health, until death."

We prefer the illusion of life and love to real life and love, and we do not abide the shattering of these illusions. Nonetheless, they are shattered in midlife and beyond, as we lose our health and bodily functions; as we lose our roles and the identities that accompany them; as we lose those we love; and in a very real sense, we lose our very selves, the selves we have created. We cannot avoid this dis-solutionment or dis-illusionment as we age, just as we could not avoid the cherished illusions about the one we love, about which we were not even aware. As Spanish philosopher Miguel de Unamuno put it: "Love is the child of illusion, and the parent of disillusion."[4] While we live in denial, our lives, too, are the children of illusion that will inevitably parent disillusion!

When this time comes in the second half of life, if not before, we have the chance to respond and fulfill our vocation that has always been calling out to us, the voice to which we turned a deaf ear because of our denial, our remaining asleep to it. Because of this unconscious decision, we have missed a lot.

We missed the experience of the moment in the here and now. In my example of mindless eating and drinking, imagine, instead, the wonderful anticipation created by the sound of the cork being pulled from the bottle of wine you selected for the meal. After pouring the wine, imagine appreciating the sight of the wine's deep, ruby red color. You spend leisurely time enjoying the wine's smell, its fruity nose, its fragrance. You savor the glass of red wine you just drank, the taste that required many hours of sunlight, rain, and the careful hand of the winemaker, the texture of the silky, smooth liquid that in some cases is called "the nectar of the gods."

Perhaps that is why we clink glasses before we take the first sip. The ritual is necessary so that the wine appeals to all the senses, the clink adding sound to the other four senses already experienced—sight, smell, taste, and touch—to add the final sense to the experience and to give us its fullness. I believe there is another reason. It is intended to make us mindful of what we are about to do, about that which is happening and is about to happen. It is a wake-up call, a call to experience the fullness of the moment, the greater fullness of life that has been buried in the sleep of our denial.

Why do we want to stay asleep?
Carol Orsborn

To become wise you must learn to listen to the wild dogs barking in your cellar.
NIETZSCHE

I thought I had the answer to this question and began to write. But in the midst of mulling it over, I was faced with a near tragedy. My husband's and my beloved dog Lucky, an eight pound maltese-yorky mix, was viciously attacked by a giant German shepherd. Lucky was on leash, my husband and Lucky lagging a few steps behind me. Unbeknownst to any of us, the predator lay in wait under a bench while his owner ate lunch at an outdoor café. I felt a tug on the leash, and as I whirled around I heard my husband shouting, screams from passersby, and most terrifying of all, Lucky's howl, then—and this was even more horrifying—her silence. It took Dan and another man ten long seconds to pry the shepherd's jaws open and for Lucky to be released to my arms. Lucky was seriously wounded, but given proper care, and living up to her name, she has bounced back to her joyful self. But why I'm writing about this now is what happened in the midst of the attack, when I saw Lucky's little body gripped helplessly in the jaws of the beast and realized that she might already be dead.

As I process this incident, I understand that my reaction of horror at the prospect of losing her was entirely normal. However, having faced death previously with my own diagnosis and treatment of breast cancer eighteen years ago, I thought I'd long ago made peace with mortality. Apparently I had not.

As if Lucky's encounter weren't wake-up call enough to my unprocessed anxiety, I realize that I had not yet truly dealt with the difficult deaths of a number of people whose spirituality over the decades had served as beacons of inspiration and hope for me. The first was Diane Caughey, my Los Angeles spiritual counselor. The second was John Mogabgab, friend and editor to Henri Nouwen, and husband of my long-term Nashville spiritual companion and guide, author Marjorie Thompson. The third was the passing at age eighty-nine of Rabbi Zalman Schachter-Shalomi, author of the seminal work *From Age-ing to Sage-ing: A Profound New Vision of Growing Older*. One of the pioneers of the conscious aging movement, Reb Zalman's health challenges, spiritual struggles, and triumphs were chronicled during the "December" years of his life by writer Sara Davidson in her book *The December Project: An Extraordinary Rabbi and a Skeptical Seeker Confront Life's Greatest Mystery*.

Aspects of each of these deaths—even beyond the relatively young ages of John and Diane and the suddenness of the trajectory of John's illness—caught me off-guard, reminding me that spiritual maturity, while an end in and of itself, cannot always be counted on to mitigate pain and suffering.

Processing the difficult deaths of three of the most spiritual people I have encountered, I am that much more aware that my time on Earth—under the best of circumstances—is limited, and more to the point, that even my spiritual resources are no sort of guarantee that I can avoid doubts, pain, and suffering.

I am older now than when I received my breast cancer diagnosis and the passage of time has made a difference. I now realize that as serious as it was, breast cancer was something from which I could at least hope to recover. I could hope to benefit from the prayers of others, as well as my own. But aging, on the other hand, is not something from which any of us can ever hope to recover. The stakes have been raised as my spiritual fantasies are put to ever bigger tests. I wish I could turn the clock back to the time I truly believed that I could never be faced by anything that could not be overcome by prayer and positive thinking, but aging is making the illusion of immortality harder and harder to maintain.

"Why do we want to stay asleep?" Perhaps because the whole truth is often more than we can bear. There are times when we not only want, but perhaps need, the comfort of living in the present moment, simply putting one foot ahead of the other in order to make it through the day, not seeking meaning nor struggling for answers.

But in the end, long term, there is a price that is paid in the effort to turn our backs on ultimate concerns. Are there those among us who throw ourselves into reinvented careers not because we need the money, or even because we are fueled by passion, but rather, because we are driven by the fear that our moment of vital contribution will have otherwise passed us by? Does the driven ambition to leave a lasting legacy stem from the sincere desire to make a difference or the anxious concern that otherwise we will be forgotten?

In fact, existential philosopher Rollo May and psychotherapist Irvin Yalom contend that all of our anxiety, from how our children are faring to whether or not we'll outlast our savings, stems from a deeper and more universal source than we'd normally ascribe. In brief, the everyday dramas that threaten to sweep us through the years beyond midlife are little more than stand-ins for what it is that is really bothering us: the deeply held universal fear about the extinction of existence at the end of life. This is a fear so onerous, it attaches itself like a chameleon to something—anything, in fact—over which we at least have the illusion of control. As uncomfortable as this is, it is preferable to facing what we're really terrified of: nothingness.

Anxiety about our adult children and grandchildren, for instance, may seem to be about whether they're financially stable, finding the right mate, and raising happy, successful children themselves. Of course, there is a degree of concern that is normal and natural in regard to our feelings about those for whom we care. But when there is an excessive, irrational expression of anxiety, it is a signal to look deeper and see if our concerns are, in fact, an antidote to our fear of death—hoping against hope for immortality through our offspring. Anxieties about our financial futures can be traced to similar roots. For instance, do we resist budgeting now as part of planning for the future because in doing so, we are forced to confront the finitude of our lives? Do we cringe at the financial planner's question "How long do you plan to live?"—or do we avoid the planning process entirely, knowing that this question of finite lifespan is one that is begging to be addressed? Do we have trouble making choices, let alone commitments, because in doing so, we view our life as one of diminishing rather than expanding possibilities? In the face of mortal fear, we want to stay asleep simply because waking up is so utterly painful.

So why wake up at all?

As Sogyal Rinpoche writes in *The Tibetan Book of Living and Dying:* "When we finally know we are dying, and all other sentient beings are dying with us, we start to have a burning, almost heartbreaking sense of the fragility and preciousness of each moment and each being, and from this can grow a deep, clear, limitless compassion for all beings."[5]

Rinpoche instructs us to live deep, strong, and full as we free ourselves from victimhood to the passage of time to instead become fierce with age. Short of this, our everyday anxieties keep us flailing at the surface of things, whipped here and there by deeper currents we do not even know have us in their grip.

Yes, the wild dogs are barking in the basement, but so, too, are beloved pets like Lucky emerging from the jaws of the beast to once again lick the noses of their loving masters.

The truth is that life is mysterious, awe-some, and awe-ful, all at once. In the end we wake up because we can only be fully alive to the degree to which we are willing to become aware of the enormity of existence.

Question 7
What wakes you up?
Carol Orsborn

Earlier we spoke of disillusionment as the entryway to spiritual growth: a turn toward rather than away from the uncomfortable and unresolved issues in our life. The pain of turning toward that which we previously had been able to evade is not an apathetic act of resignation. The Greek root from which the word *apathy* derives actually means the avoidance, not the experience, of suffering. In fact, peeling away layers of illusion to confront what Eastern philosophy and Western mystics alike experience as "nothingness" turns out to be the very ground in which awakening can most readily take root. Writer Dorothy Lessing puts it like this: "Almost all men . . . have strange imaginings.

The strangest of these is a belief that they can progress only by improvement. Those who understand will realize that we are much more in need of stripping off than adding on."[6]

Crisis foils our expectations, shakes us out of the false security of the status quo, and carries the potential to wake us up. Sooner or later everybody comes face to face with challenge, change, and uncertainty. And yet, being met with crisis can't be the whole answer to the question "What Wakes You Up," because we all know plenty of people to whom bad things have happened and who yet manage to miss out on the opportunity for transformation. It turns out that when we come face to face with the unwanted issues of our lives, despite the potential for spiritual advancement, we have options. We can ignore the situation, as does the spouse who continues to live with an abusive partner, literally turning the other cheek. She may rationalize denial by telling herself and others stories about the situation: "He loves me, and is only hitting me because he cares so much." Any of us can become passive victims of circumstances, anesthetizing ourselves with interpretations that belie common sense, as well as anything that will help us dull the pain: drugs, alcohol, addictions of any type. But simply reacting to challenge and pain with big emotion does not necessarily mean that one has broken denial to live a more authentic life. It is possible, too, to run and rerun dramas of victimization, giving the impression that one is facing one's shadows energetically, while in truth proactively fending off anything that even begins to hint of awakening.

On the other hand there are those of us who allow ourselves to become transformed by whatever comes our way. Thomas Merton in *The Silent Life* describes one who has allowed life's challenges to awaken him: "He can peacefully accept that when his false ideas of himself are gone he has practically nothing else left. But then he is ready for the encounters with reality: The Truth and the Holiness of God, which he must learn to confront in the depths of his own nothingness."[7]

So why is it that some people become reactive or diminished in the face of challenge and change, while others can find in themselves the determination to live life that much more fully and consciously? One could respond that it is a fortunate confluence of psychological and spiritual influences, perhaps traced back to early life: supportive parents, a meaningful religious upbringing, a genetic disposition toward consciousness, hard psycho-spiritual work, or just plain good luck. But then, too, we all know at least several who hail from the same background and genetic pool: those who make the choice to stay hidden beneath a veil of denial, while the others allow themselves to be awakened to the larger, more meaningful embrace of the whole of life. What wakes the latter up while the former sleepwalks through it all?

During the many years I pursued first my master's of theological studies, then my doctorate in the history and critical theory of religion, it was this line of inquiry that captured the essence of both my intellectual and personal quest. What wakes us up? Is it free will? Is it grace? Is there an alternative yet to be revealed? It was only when I encountered the notions that comprise the heart of process theology that I found an explanation that seemed both possible and appealing to me, an understanding that helped me make sense of everything.

Stated as simply as possible, my answer is that waking up is a personal choice—but one that we are eternally persuaded toward by the Divine. We are, indeed, the product of everything that has ever happened to us, including the potential to make both the worst and the best possible choices at any moment. The message of hope I discovered in process theology, and that resonates with me at the deepest levels, is that there is, however, a built-in bias for the good. I think of this bias as God and view my relationship to the Divine as one in which I am both free to make my own choices and simultaneously urged in the direction of transformation. Many influences contribute to what we choose for ourselves, and among these influences, hope, faith, courage, generosity, curiosity and all of the qualities we associate with psycho-spiritual health play a role. Perhaps it is a very small consideration, but even one's intention to live a more fully realized life may carry just enough weight to make the difference.

In *Journey to Emptiness: Dogen, Merton, Jung and the Quest for Transformation,* author Robert Jingen Gunn writes that our experience of emptiness takes us "to the exact edge of life and death. . . . There we are forced to make a choice about how to live: whether to follow vitality with its attendant risks, struggles and promise, or whether to succumb to the death within life of unconsciousness."[8]

It is our very yearning to expand to embrace the wider potential of the human experience including compassion, bittersweet sadness, and yes, even profound happiness, that holds the potential to wake us up. Awakening is always an option. Even when we can merely hope to awaken, we are making the choice to respond to the Divine urging us toward accepting that while pain is inescapable, so, too, is God.

What wakes you up?
Bob Weber

For the past year, on most days, I have been waking up without an alarm at the same time every morning, 5:45 a.m. In part it is due to a shift in my circadian rhythms that has come with aging—but that is only part of the reason.

What is interesting is that roughly four years ago I turned sixty-five and began Medicare—two significant milestones. Perhaps I am just experiencing the commonly held belief that older people do not need as much sleep. (Did I just say "older people" and include myself in that cohort? After all, sixty-five is the long-accepted age for being old in our country! I suspect that it has to do with a yet unarticulated awareness of where I am in the course of my life—and anticipated death.)

My experience is that people, things, and events can all keep me in a state of sleep because of the illusions with which they can enthrall me. Cheng-Li, a Buddhist, put it well:

"You sentient beings who seek deliverance, why do you not let go? When sad, let go of the cause of sadness. . . . When covetous or lustful, let go of the object of desire. From moment to moment be free of self. Where no self is, there can be no sorrow, no desire. . . . The winds of circumstance blow across emptiness. Whom can they harm?"[9]

At the same time that each person, thing, and event can lull me into sleep, they can also awaken me. Let me give the most important, continual example of the one "who" wakes me up. This is my wife, Pamela.

And this is not because she awakens me in the morning. In fact, she is a late-night person, capable of reading for hours into the night, while I doze off after two or three pages. As a result she typically awakens later than I in the morning. This is not bad since our rhythms afford us alone time that she and I, all of us, need on a daily basis.

Prior to my marriage my Jesuit life certainly awakened me to many realities, material and spiritual. What I did not know was how much my life partner would awaken me to truths about myself that were never fully revealed, even during my time as a Jesuit who was trying "to find God in all things." Turns out, through marriage I was given a person through whom the divinity speaks, who continually says, "Bob, Wake up! Wake up!"

There are many ways she has awakened me to life, probably the most important of which is a much, much deeper appreciation of the meaning of love as an act of surrender to another, not just a submissive resignation. This awakening enabled me to overcome my fear of a loss of my very self in loving another—the fruit of which is a most remarkably fulfilling life.

Of the many other awakenings I could list and elaborate, I want to focus on how Pamela wakes me up to the importance of "letting go," letting go of the many things I hold—possessions, attitudes, bad habits, obsessions—but which, in fact, have a more powerful hold on me. These things, events, and people restrict my freedom and extract an exorbitant price in terms of my time, my health, and my well-being, physically and spiritually. Recall Cheng-Li's comment above—"let go."

A simple, frequently occurring example has to do with my driving. Boston and Cambridge are notoriously strenuous and stressful cities to navigate by car. Drivers are, more often than not, impatient and quick to anger, not unlike me. Pamela continually reminds me that not only is this not good for me and upsetting to her, but it is also inconsistent with the religious and spiritual values I purport to embrace, like loving your neighbor. At such moments I "wake up" to the fact that I profess certain beliefs, and she, while not professing them, lives them far better than I do. Her oft-repeated remark is "That's really Christian of you!" She encourages me to let go of what I hold on to, which holds on to me.

In addition to being a psychologist, my wife is a cabaret singer. Among her many great renditions of songs is her recorded performance of "Let It Be" by the Beatles.[10] Her interpretation and delivery capture the essence of the marriage of music and lyrics embodied in the song. It remains a compelling reminder of her oft-repeated admonition to "let it be." Such words of wisdom, just let it be!

Question 8

Has there been a particular experience that has finally awakened you?

Bob Weber

Currently, when I ask myself, "What wakes me up?" I am not sure I want to wake up. If we envision every awakening as a beautiful sunrise in the morning, we are probably fooling ourselves and remaining in denial. Some wake-up calls are "rude awakenings" that we would rather not experience. Why that is so will become clearer as you read on.

While responding to this question about "waking up," I am aware that my Catholic tradition's liturgical season of Lent is in full swing. Lent is a season of awakening before the Easter feast and celebration of the resurrection. It is mirrored by the pre-Christmas season of Advent that is heralded by hymns such as *"Wachet Auf!" "Wake Up!"*

When I was a kid, the question was always, "What are you giving up for Lent?" My father gave up cigarettes, and I would give up candy or some other pleasure in order to develop a Lenten, penitential spirit. Over the years the tradition changed, and now the question is not what will you give up but what will you do for others, such as, for example, take that candy money and donate it to an organization that serves others.

This year my Lenten observance is not about "doing" anything, not giving up this or that, not about contributing to a worthy cause—it is about "being" with, surrendering to the realities I now face in the hope of growing and maturing, spiritually. Let me elaborate.

One of Lent's traditional readings, proclaimed during the second Sunday of Lent, has become the basis for my Lenten meditation. In the Gospels of Matthew, Mark, and Luke, the story of "the transfiguration" is pivotal to the spiritual maturation of the Christ's followers. As his followers are getting to know him, they become more and more hopeful that he is the messianic figure who will return Israel to its former glory days. He will become the new King David, and they will be part of his lofty inner circle. They envision victory, glory, power, status, and prestige for themselves.

This vision is only reinforced for Peter, James, and John when, after they ascend the mountain and reach its summit, Jesus is transfigured, made glorious in appearance. Overwhelmed, Peter says, "It is good for us to be here!" and wants to remain there, at the peak. However, just as quickly, the transfiguration ends, and the foursome heads back down the mountain, back to the drudgery and reality of daily life. Shortly after the descent Jesus disabuses all the followers of their grandiose, messianic vision. He tells them that he will be arrested and killed. Peter tries to persuade him to avoid this fate; however, Christ chastises Peter for tempting him to avoid the realities he must face.

As a result doubts about the meaningfulness of this path abound among the followers. Even after his death and resurrection, despondency and hopelessness continue to prevail. Two disciples on their way home from Jerusalem, like Peter, had hoped for a very different path for Jesus and themselves. As he did with Peter, when he joined the two on their return to Emmaus, Jesus upbraids them and tries to restore their hope by enlightening them about the meaning of all that has happened.

I, too, am descending the mount of the transfiguration. I, too, am on the road to Emmaus. Recent events in my own life have put me on a parallel path. My life is better than it has ever been (save for the myriad physical aches, pains, and problems that are emerging as I enter my sixty-ninth year). In a very real sense my own life has been "transfigured," as I have found the path to a way of being and working in the world that speaks about who I am at deeper and deeper levels.

Like the followers on their way down the mountain, I, too, got the "bad news." A prostate biopsy was recommended to rule out malignancy. This has cast a shadowy cloud over my sunlit life and has provoked anxiety and fear. In the process of assessing my situation, I have been diligent, practicing "active surveillance," gathering all the information I can, and speaking to all the people I know who have been through this before, to calm myself and to make an informed decision about which course of action to pursue. Nonetheless, I am not above fear and early morning, sweaty awakenings—"rude awakenings"—have occurred.

This is my descent from the mountain and into the dark night of the soul. This descent has invited me to make a "leap of faith," a belief that what is occurring is meaning-full, not without meaning. I do not know what I will find out about life and myself as I navigate these stormy waters. I am not yet sure what the final word will be. In the meantime I will practice "watchful waiting."

What I hope for is a faith-filled surrender to life as it is emerging. This is not a submission, nor a passive acceptance of defeat. It is an embrace of all that life and death are. It is a belief that something more is, has been, and always will be going on and that my life is embedded in this foundational reality, which for me is God. Hopefully, I can say as Jesus did at the moment of his death, confidently, "Into your hands I commit my spirit."

Has there been a particular experience that has finally awakened you?

Carol Orsborn

Many years ago, when I was in the heart of my marketing career, I had a sudden, most unwelcome awakening. I had thought that I was an excellent boss, beloved by my staff. But one day I stumbled onto a staff meeting that had not been called by me, but as it turned out, had been called by the staff about me to formalize their multiple complaints. At that moment I was suddenly and rudely awakened from the illusions of my youth. It was painful to learn so suddenly that I was not the master of the universe I'd come to believe. But it was also the crisis that first awakened me to a fuller understanding of what it could mean to be more fully alive.

This was an important moment of awakening for me, but was it definitive? Thinking over the course of my life, much of it captured in journals, I began remembering many such moments of painful awakening. Journal after journal, there were twenty years of unexpected change, challenge, and uncertainty: crises of faith, the brush with breast cancer, children leaving the nest, job loss, and so on and on, each one culminating with a profound new level of awareness.

I don't believe that Bob and I intended this as a trick question when we crafted it. But the experience of revisiting the past forty years of my spiritual life turns out to be both humbling and illuminating. And so it is that I arrive at last at the answer to this question: "no." There was not a particular experience that finally awakened me. In fact, and perhaps this says more about my own recalcitrant nature than about spiritual growth in general, I have discovered a repetitive pattern in my process of awakening that defies the notion of a onetime transformation, conversion, or any other term that implies something definitive, fixed, and permanent.

For me awakening is more along the lines of a spiral, an awareness that rises and falls on a subtly ascending curve. At the peak of each upward movement of the spiral is a breakthrough akin to the notion of awakening. Like the phases of the moon, however, this is followed by a gentle and gradual dimming of the illumination. At the trough I find that it often appears that I have forgotten what just days or months ago seemed so clear and am back exactly where I started, once again fast asleep. Of course this is not true. For between one trough and the next, there have been life lessons, added experiences, and a growing bank of resources from which to draw. I may, in fact I do, experience this trough as hitting bottom over and over again— but having had many such cycles under my belt, I have the added perspective that this time is, at least, a higher bottom than last.

While Zen philosophy posits the notion of a sudden awakening, the theory that most resembles my own experience finds its roots in another branch of the Eastern tradition: the I Ching, or Book of Changes. Taking its cue from the cycles of nature, the I Ching describes growing awareness as an expanding spiral, each turn of the spiral grown stronger, larger, fed by the enriched soil of one's experiences. There is growth; there is progress. But it is an advancement, not despite our challenges, setbacks, and backsliding, but including them.[11]

Even now, and sometimes, especially now, I have times when I feel lost and hopeless, wandering in the abyss. But I also have something added: the understanding that for me being awake simply means that I have made a choice—somewhere along the way and then over and over again—to live as if everything that is happening to me, the good and the bad, is happening within God's embrace. At times the best I can muster is to celebrate how far I've come to at least be awake enough to know when I am asleep. This I can attest to definitively. And happily, it is a start.

Question 9

What do you think the Sacred wants to awaken you to?

Carol Orsborn

My friend and fellow spiritual guide Rabbi Dayle Friedman is one of the leading experts on spirituality and aging. Having served as a rabbi for a community of 1,100 elders living in a nursing home and supportive-living apartment complex, it was her privilege to accompany her congregants through the final stretch of their journey through life. Along the way she provided them with spiritual support through illness, loss, learning, celebrating, and ultimately, the ends of their lives. From her front-row seat facing the realities of aging day after day, she found strength in a teaching of the Kabbalah that also helps me to form my answer to the profound question: What do I think God wants to awaken me to?

The teaching from the Kabbalah centers on the concept

of *Shever v'Tikkun:* "shattering and redemption," as taught by Rabbi Isaac Luria, the beloved sixteenth-century mystic and sage known as "the Ari." According to the Ari, before creation, God's light was abundant and omnipresent. God's first act was to create vessels to bring form and substance out of the light to be the world. But through "a devastating cosmic accident," so powerful was God's light that it could not be contained in the vessels. The vessels shattered into tiny pieces and the sparks of light became encased in shards. The shards of light were concealed in a world of darkness. Writes Rabbi Friedman: "Our human task is to find and to liberate those sparks, and thus bring repair (tikkun) and redemption to this broken existence."[12]

Earlier I spoke of my own awakening not as one definitive moment that transformed the darkness into light. My conception of what God wants to awaken us to is much more aligned with the notion of *tikkun:* the redemption of meaning, light, and goodness. When we adopt this as our responsibility, we accept that it is our personal sacred task to find and redeem the light from where there was once darkness. We do this every time we have compassion for ourselves or others, every time we feel gratitude for what we have been given, every time we replace arrogance with humility, and every time we stifle the urge to say or do something that persists in keeping the light hidden and dispersed when we could have, instead, contributed to the work of repair.

"One becomes aware of the profound responsibility and immense task of repairing the world, understanding that this is a lifelong work that takes place one shard at a time. Tikkun happens every time we turn to tell the truth about our own as well as the world's fears, shadows, pains, and shortcomings, and make the choice about how we are going to respond. We can dwell in the darkness, becoming victims of the world's as well as our own brokenness. Or we can seek to liberate the sparks of light hidden in even the darkest moments. We do this every time we rise above reactivity to the moment to ground ourselves in that which is enduring, transcendent, and nourishing."[13] This is tikkun.

To illustrate tikkun, Rabbi Friedman shares the story of "Wilma," who was paralyzed by a stroke at the age of seventy-two. Despite her disability she made everyone her friend, greeting everybody by name and sharing her irrepressible spirit. When a second stroke left her unable to speak and totally paralyzed, she nevertheless found ways to communicate. She learned to speak by pointing, spelling out words on an alphabet board. Rabbi Friedman would ask Wilma, "How's it going?" Wilma would shape her fingers into the "OK" sign. The Rabbi would ask her if she would be going to worship services. Wilma would point to the ceiling, her sign for "God willing." When it was time to say goodbye, Wilma would always sign, "I love you." Writes Rabbi Friedman: "In the face of hardships that would prompt most people to withdraw in anger or frustration, Wilma remained distinctly herself. She found ways to draw others to her with love, creativity, and passion. She sought—and found—the holy sparks and illuminated the darkness for all she touched."[14]

Mystics and seekers from many traditions yearn to transcend everyday reality to live in God's never-ending light, embraced by bliss. We wish awakening was not such a lifelong challenge, retrieving bits of light from the shadows one shard at a time. But in the words of Thomas Merton: when one is ready for the encounters with reality "what one finds . . . is not a collection of great mystics and men of dazzling spiritual gifts, but simple and rugged souls whose mysticism is all swallowed up in a faith too big and too simple for visions."[15]

What do you think the Sacred wants to awaken you to?

Bob Weber

Karen Horney, a preeminent Austrian psychoanalyst of the early twentieth century, left her home one morning and headed to the railroad station in Vienna. She went to catch a train for another city where she was delivering a keynote talk to her colleagues. As she headed to the gate, two minutes late, she experienced what many American travelers who are unfamiliar with European rail services discover: punctuality! The train was already departing—right on time! Horney's emotional response to this was outrage, and her verbal response, "Don't you know who I am!?"

It is said that Horney developed, in that moment, a much deeper experience of the meaning of a psychoanalytic concept not unfamiliar to her, narcissism: in this case, her own! Now, narcissism is not a bad or evil phenomenon; in fact, a healthy narcissism is essential for our development as human beings. Heinz Kohut, an American analyst, writes beautifully about the necessary progressions for developing healthy narcissism in the elaboration of his theory of self-psychology.[16]

We have all had the opportunity to interact with a little baby who engages us and we her with eyes, smiles, and gurgling sounds or big puffs of breath. We both sense the pleasure contained in such a moment. For the baby this is "mirroring." The little one sees herself mirrored by us and in this way becomes more her-SELF, visible to and recognized by another, us. Without this something crucial is missing, and we are compelled to seek it again and again, driven by something about which we may not even be aware.

For example, Johnny Carson, famous for the *Tonight Show,* was admired for his role as the program's master of ceremonies. He gave others room to shine in his presence, and he, himself, stood out and shone for his wit and humor. Nonetheless, there was one person who never gave him the admiration and mirroring his audiences did: his mother. On one occasion she watched his show, and a news commentator asked what she thought of it. Her response was, "It was not very funny." Apparently, her failure to mirror him was prevalent from childhood onward. Johnny's older sister was the apple of his mother's eye, so despite his lifelong attempts to evoke what he needed from her in many important ways, it was never forthcoming.

In Kohut's model of human development, a second experience is also crucial, "idealizing." By this Kohut means that a person needs to idealize and participate in the greatness of another in order to become himself.[17] For me that idealized figure was my father. I received his mirroring and tried to become what he dreamed I would become. I wanted to be like him and admired his ability to work with his hands as a carpenter and mechanic; however, he dissuaded me from doing such work and, instead, encouraged me to study hard and succeed through a college education. He also envisioned me as a priest, and as I have written in an earlier section, for a lengthy period I tried to fulfill his wish and his dream for me.

So what does this digression into psychological theory have to do with the question, "What do you think God wants to awaken you to?" At the heart of Kohut's vision of human development is an awareness of the deep yearning in all of us to be seen, protected, comforted, and loved for who we are. It has taken me more than sixty years to begin to appreciate and more deeply experience this reality in my life.

At times it bothers me that it has taken so long and that it is still becoming, but has not yet solidified as, a truth that enables me to relax a bit more. Nonetheless, I take heart because others whom I admire, like Mother Teresa and Henri Nouwen, the Dutch priest and prolific spiritual writer, struggled with this to the end as well. Nouwen's mantra could have been "You are the beloved of God," for it pervades and infuses his writings. During an invited sermon at Robert Schuller's Crystal Cathedral, Nouwen drove this point home again and again, and seemed to be doing so as much for himself as his audience.[18] To the end of his life, Nouwen was driven to seek the love of God and the love of others. His own dark side(s) and self-doubts fueled this quest as they do or have for many of us. While I believe that I will still have moments when I anxiously wonder how lovable I really am in the eyes of my God, I am now at a point in my life where I am much more accepting of the fact that I am "beloved of God."

This fundamental truth is what I now understand that God has been and continues to be trying to awaken me to. When it touches the depths of my being, I am able to radiate a smile of peace and joy!

Question 10

Is there a constructive role for regret, shame, and guilt?

Bob Weber

Webster defines *denial* as "a refusal to admit the truth or reality." In psychological jargon denial is a defense mechanism. It serves a person by buffering her from a painful or burdensome reality. In my psychotherapeutic work with patients, I often rename it a self-protective mechanism to highlight its intent: to protect. I also emphasize that facing and grappling with the realities that confront us is the only pathway to psychological growth and maturation. However, this facing of reality must be done with attention to the pace of the particular person. There is no "one-size-fits-all."

For example, Elisabeth Kubler-Ross writes that the first response to the death of a loved one is denial. "He's not really dead!" is an attempt to stave off the onslaught of grief unleashed by the loss. Eventually, however, in order to get on with life and attain some degree of freedom from the impact of the harsh truth, a person must face the reality of the loss and do the "grief work," that is, grieve in the face of the reality of the loss, the bereavement, the being stripped of the relationship.

While it is essential to grieve, it may be necessary to delay the grief work in order to carry on, temporarily. When my father died I used "selective inattention" to cope with the situation so that I could attend to the work that needed to be done in order to arrange his funeral. Selective inattention is a coping mechanism, in contrast to denial, which is a defense mechanism. While denial and other defense mechanisms are by their nature automatic and unconscious, selective inattention and other coping mechanisms are intentional and conscious. In effect, the latter are made in a state of awakeness, the former while asleep and unconscious.

Spiritual growth, too, demands that we face the realities of life and of ourselves—the sometimes unwanted realities of our lives, for example, pain and suffering, disappointment, losses that cause us regret, and the unwanted truths about ourselves that cause us guilt and shame. At moments when we are beset by regret or guilt or shame, we have choices to make. As we have said previously, such times can be opportunities for psychological and spiritual growth. They are occasions of "crisis."

The word *crisis* strikes an unwanted chord in us, one that is foreboding and ominous. However, the word *crisis* derives from the Greek language and means "a time of decision." In effect, every crisis is also an opportunity to wake up and live more freely. At times of crisis we may regret the circumstances and earlier decisions we made that got us into the crisis.

In the very first chapter of her book, *The Gift of Years: Growing Old Gracefully,* Joan Chittister writes this about regret:

> The burden of regret is that, unless we come to understand the value of the choices we made in the past, we may fail to see the gifts they have brought us.
>
> The blessing of regret is clear—it brings us, if we are willing to face it head on, to the point of being present to this new time of life in an entirely new way. It urges us on to continued becoming.[19]

Crises invite us to make choices that enable us to continue "becoming." This is the core of the spiritual life, to continue becoming our "true selves." As the existential philosophers put it, we are "being-in-becoming," who by our freedom to choose and by the decisions we make become who we really are at the deepest levels and in the eyes of God.

But we cannot wake up and set aside denial until we are prepared and ready to face ourselves. Guilt and shame are emotions that wake us up to the truth of ourselves, and they are not pleasant wake-up calls. Both tell us that we are not all that we may think we are. Shame and guilt injure our egos and deflate our narcissism. Guilt tells us that we "did" something bad or wrong. Shame tells us that I "am" sometimes a bad person, capable of doing something bad.

Our reaction to both guilt and shame is to push back at them and to push them away. When I was about the age of ten and my sister was roughly five, I was reprimanded by my mother for teasing my sister. Retrospectively, I can truly say that I had been mean and cruel in my words and actions toward her. However, at the time I denied that I did anything wrong. I wanted to remain the unashamed, good boy and apple of my mother's eye.

None of us wants to lose face or be ashamed in the eyes of others, which is why the feeling of shame, even more than guilt, makes us feel mortified such that we wish we could fall off the face of the Earth in order to avoid being seen so by others. The truth is that, at times, we do things that are bad and we are bad, at times, just as we can do good things and are good, essentially. The real truth is we are both saints and sinners.

If we do not face this truth about ourselves, but instead choose to run and hide from ourselves, the guilt and the shame will get the better of us and send us on a downward spiral of hopelessness and despair. To avoid this we must break denial, face the truth of ourselves in all its aspects, those welcome and those unwelcome, and grieve the loss of our idealized, false image of ourselves.

To understand what I am saying, let us consider the stories of Peter and Judas. Both eventually denied and betrayed Jesus. Peter, rather than despairing, "wept bitterly" over what he had done and returned to face the man he denied, repentant and remorseful. In contrast, Judas despaired and hanged himself. He, like Peter, would have been forgiven even for his betrayal had he only been able to bear his guilt and shame. We can only guess that the injuries to his ego, and narcissism, held the day, whereas Peter's were battered by his actions, and he faced the truth about himself, dismantling a probably grandiose image of himself as a man. In the end he was able to face Jesus, the man he denied publicly, and look him in the eye with sorrow and regret in his own heart.

King David (1 Kings) also faced such a pivotal moment that could have gone either way. Here was a man destined for greatness, the man who slew the Philistine giant, Goliath, and led Israel into a period of greatness. He had everything: position, esteem, possessions, and wealth. Nonetheless, he wanted the wife of one of his soldiers, Uriah's Bathsheba, and he took her, sending Uriah off to be killed in battle, fighting for him.

Nathan the prophet very tactfully confronted David and his actions by telling the story of an Israelite, one of David's subjects, who took possession of his tenant's one and only prized sheep and then killed the man. David, outraged by Nathan's report, asked Nathan to reveal the man to him so he might pass judgment on him. Nathan replied to David's request by saying, "That man is you!" David, to his credit, faced this truth, put on sackcloth and ashes, and publicly repented for what he had done rather than denying what happened to save face.

This is what we, too, must do to be free. Shame and guilt are like mildew, which does very well in the darkness, proliferating when hidden from sunlight, destroying the material on which it is growing. Breaking denial is bringing such feelings out into the light. To make it a real experience, we must admit it to ourselves. Further light emerges when we choose to tell another, a friend, a therapist, a confessor, minister, priest, or rabbi. And we can look directly into God's eyes through prayer and be unburdened and freer.

Is there a constructive role for regret, shame, and guilt?

Carol Orsborn

Encountering a 2012 issue of *AARP The Magazine* online, I read words by Bette Midler that illustrate the constructive role of facing regret, shame, and guilt. After a lifelong wrestle with her shadows, she was asked to share "What I Know Now." Her answer: "Life is not your personal express lane. You've got to figure, well, there are 7 billion other people in the world. It doesn't all have to be about me. It took me about 66 years to come to this conclusion."[20] As Bette's story reveals, a certain degree of introspection is healthy. But as the old saying goes, while the unexamined life is a life not worth living, the over-examined life is not living, at all.

In the book Bob cited earlier, *The Gift of Years: Growing Older Gracefully,* author Joan Chittister cites the positive potential of regret to lead to self-awareness, but can also function as "a sand trap of the soul," which "comes upon us one day dressed up like wisdom, looking profound and serious, sensible and responsible." But this, Joan points out, is in reality a temptation and a misuse of the aging process, sapping our valuable energy by turning our attention to fantasy centering on what could have been. "Regret claims to be insight. But how can it be spiritual insight to deny the good of what has been for the sake of what was not?" Joan teaches that "there are many ways to fullness of life, all of them different, all of them unique."[21]

In order to get on with our lives, we have to confront the discomforting truth that we may never know why we made the choices we did, why we got the unlucky family or set of circumstances. And even more so that no amount of introspection may provide us with the means to rectify it all. Once we give up the notion that we can be masters of the universe, we free ourselves from enslavement of the past and move into the present. Joan writes:

> One of the functions—one of the gifts—of aging is to become comfortable with the self we are, rather than to mourn what we are not . . . it is a moment of great enlightenment when we realize that the years have grown us as well as sustained us. We are of more substance now than we were when we were young, whatever we did in the past, wherever we were when we did it. The fact is that twinges of regret are a step-over point in life. They invite us to revisit the ideals and motives that brought us to where we are now.[22]

When, at last, you are at the point of having made amends for everything of the past that is rectifiable and have become firmly committed to addressing new causes for remorse in the present moment, then you stop living your life by looking only in the rearview mirror and point your nose back toward the heat of life.

6

What Is Freedom?

11. What illusions does aging dispel?

12. Which illusions are the most difficult to let go?

13. Is there a positive purpose to keeping some of our illusions?

14. What does it mean to be free in light of the ebbing of physicality and social connection?

15. What still keeps you at the mercy of particular events, things, and people?

THE QUESTION OF FREEDOM

For years, when market researchers asked boomers if they'd like to retire someday, the answer was no. But ask us what quality we most value and would like more of in our lives, and the answer has been unmistakable: we want to be free. Since the sixties ours has been a generation of men and women who have elevated the ability to make choices, defy the status quo, and determine our own destinies to the top of the list of aspirations. We've been pushing the envelope through all manner of life stages and ages and have no intention of stopping now that we're passing beyond midlife into the next phase of our lives. In fact, if anything, our taste for calling our own shots has reached an all-time high. Now, whether boomers intend to continue working, anticipate retiring, or invent our own unique blend of the two, one thing is for sure: we aim to have more freedom in our lives.

But as the social scientists, psychologists, and spiritual teachers are quick to let us know, freedom is often easier to imagine than to achieve. First of all there are external factors to contend with—limitations imposed on our dreams of freedom by financial, physical, and societal constrictions. When we pass beyond midlife, it becomes increasingly important to ask yourself what being free means for you, personally, especially in light of the ebbing away of many of the attributes and illusions of youth. How do you understand the state of being free in your own life in the face of challenge and limitation?

Webster's dictionary takes us partway toward illumination. First, the meaning of the word *freedom* is contingent on the context in which the word is being used. For example, the first tier of definitions implies freedom in a sociopolitical sense: having the legal and political rights of a citizen; enjoying civil and political liberty;

or enjoying political independence or freedom from outside domi-
nation. This definition of freedom embraces the notion of "life,
liberty, and the pursuit of happiness," as embodied in the Declara-
tion of Independence and Constitution of "the land of the free."

For those of us who have remained or become more politi-
cally active as we age, we know how challenging it is to close
the gap between aspiration and reality on something as basic
and universal as "the American dream." But as difficult as it is
to wrestle with the notion of freedom in the context of external structures and forces, seeking internal freedom can be just
as or even more challenging. We struggle to shed the opinions
of others that we no longer want or need in our lives. We seek
to discover and shed limitations we've imposed upon ourselves.
We painfully confront our desperate attempts at false freedom,
coming to recognize that the promise of denial and illusion are
short-lived and that they indeed imprison us in faulty fortresses
and deaden our capacity to live life authentically.

To accomplish inner freedom it is impingent upon us to find
the courage and strength to walk a path through the ebbing tide
of the changes in our lives and times by deepening our spirituality, dismantling the illusions of escape, and, thereby, strength-
ening ourselves for the challenges ahead. This will not be easy.
However, with the solid anchorage of a spiritual life, further
developed by the very fact of aging and the unique conditions of
your own aging process, you always have the potential to come
alive again in unimaginable ways, ways easily obscured by fear,
anxiety, and the alternative illusions that denial encourages. It
is always possible, regardless of the circumstances you face, to
claim your inalienable right to be free.

Question 11
What illusions does aging dispel?
Carol Orsborn

When I was in my late thirties, the *New York Times* published an article about me and an organization I founded, Superwomen's Anonymous, which was a club for baby boomer women who were tired of trying to have, do, and be it all.[1] Attracting tens of thousands of equally exhausted women, Superwomen's Anonymous was hailed by one of the many articles and interviews that appeared in the national media as "the harbinger of things to come"—part of the pioneering work our generation contributed to the then-revolutionary notion of life-balance, simplicity, and the search for meaning.

The phone rang off the hook, and I found myself with lucrative speaking engagements, media appearances, and a book deal with a major publisher. In fact, it was just after meeting with my publisher for the first time to finalize the deal that I recall standing on Fifth Avenue, deeply breathing in the heady sense that I had secured my destiny: that through this book, I had been tapped by the gods as immortal.

To make a long story short, just before my book came out, someone else—somebody who I'm sure at the time thought that she was equally blessed—hit the media circuit with a book on pretty much the same topic. The books canceled each other out, and as any author will tell you, there's nothing more deflating to youthful illusions of immortality than walking into a bargain bookstore and seeing your life's work in the remainder bin for ninety-nine cents.

The illusion of immortality is but one of the many illusions that aging dispels. In fact, I am moved by Nobel Prize nominee Andre Malraux's assertion that: "the greatest mystery is not that we have been flung at random between the profusion of the earth and the galaxy of the stars, but that in this prison we can fashion images of ourselves sufficiently powerful to deny our nothingness."[2]

James Hollis, Ph.D., in his infinitely wise and mature *Finding Meaning in the Second Half of Life,* refers to Jung's concept of individuation from the tribe "and the deconstruction of 'the false self'" as one of the necessary, if confusing, frustrating, and disorienting initiations into true adulthood we must endure if we hope to reap the rewards of the fully lived life.[3] This initiation into psycho-spiritual maturity causes us to question and dismantle "many of the values and strategies we have derived from internalizing the dynamics and messages of our family and culture. Yet each person is invited to a new identity, new values, new attitudes toward the self and the world, which often stands in stark contrast to the life lived prior to this summons."[4]

In my case immortality was but the first of many illusions dispelled by the transit into and ultimately through midlife. On this, the other side of midlife, the deconstruction of illusions has only accelerated, as I am increasingly learning to trust that the letting go of the old, as frightening and disorienting as it may be, inevitably leads to something always profound, and occasionally stunning. As an aside, lest I lead myself—or anyone—to believe that on the other side of illusion there is certainty and peace, allow me to close with a quote from Hollis: "Psychological or spiritual development always requires a greater capacity in us for the toleration of anxiety and ambiguity. The capacity to accept this troubled state, abide it, and commit to life, is the moral measure of our maturity."[5]

What illusions does aging dispel?
Bob Weber

One of my all-time favorite cartoons is *Peanuts,* created by Charles Schultz. On one occasion Snoopy, the beagle hound, is lying on top of his doghouse after having experienced several unpleasant things. The thought bubble over his head reads, "Life is full of rude awakenings."[6]

For most, if not all of us, aging is one such "rude awakening." Our bodies tell us we are no longer what we once were, energetic young things with boundless energy and boundary-less lives yet to be lived. Our minds, once sharp as tacks, begin to fail us, and we cannot recall names or facts we could previously rattle off in an instant. Our hearts are broken more often by our very failing selves and the losses of friends, family, and finances that mount, the longer we live—and we know longevity is increasing. Our spirits can tend toward anxiety, hopelessness, and despair, which overshadow our days such that we want to just pull the covers back up over our heads when the sun rises.

Our human psyches are prepared for such moments of anxiety, fear, and dread, as they have been throughout our lives, and our self-protective defense mechanisms are deployed to shield us from these frightening, burdensome realities. Serviceable as they are in providing temporary relief from our psychological turmoil, these mechanisms constrain us in our capacity to live more freely, and they cost us dearly by robbing us of living life more fully.

Rather than allowing such experiences to reactively drive us into a besieged mentality, an "aging bunker," we can dig deeper into ourselves, into our unconscious, into our very souls, and respond by anchoring ourselves more solidly for the storm that assails us. This necessitates dispelling the illusions we have about life and ourselves and dismantling the fortifications we have fruitlessly and ineffectually constructed in an effort to protect ourselves. It requires that we face and work through the illusions, our disillusionments, and the shattered fantasies that beset us. There comes a point when we can no longer avoid or deny the fact we are going to die. No amount of Botox, bodily exercise, or other life-prolonging medications and treatments will stem this tide. Just take a good look in the mirror, as I do every morning, and take note of what is happening and what changes are occurring.

Short of the actual event of dying, we must also dispel illusions that our society and culture have fostered and cultivated—total independence, self-sufficiency, and a rugged individualism. In utero and during our early post-birth life, we are completely and absolutely dependent on our parents and others for care and well-being. As we grow up we develop capacities that allow us a modicum of power and control. We internalize culturally born attitudes that we can go it on our own, in fact, that we should be able to do so or be ashamed of ourselves. As we age we are faced with accepting our dependence on others for care and support, which we may stubbornly reject and fight off. One more illusion that aging dispels!

Question 12
Which illusions are the most difficult to let go?
Bob Weber

The core motivators that necessitate the creation of illusions are ego and pride. Earlier we considered Karen Horney's awakening to her own narcissism and her "Don't you know who I am!" Feeling privileged and special there is no question in our ego-driven minds that we have a right to go to the head of the line. We will never be last; we should never be last; and we deserve to be first. The truth is that there will never be enough to satisfy these longings in every last one of us! The fact is that we want more than anything or anyone can give! So, how do we gratify our intense ego needs? How do we feed our insatiable narcissism? What gives us pride that swells our heads?

We seek three things especially for these purposes, and not a day goes by when we do not experience some inclination to indulge one of them. These three desires provide the illusion that we are "the greatest." They are how we fool ourselves into thinking that we are better than we are, in order to offset feeling as bad and lowly as we really think we are! The three things are: (1) what I do, (2) what I have, and (3) what others say about me.

How does this work? How do we hope these three will work to satisfy us?

First, we work very hard to demonstrate how much we can do and how well we can do it—and we work very hard to surpass others in what they are doing, wherever they are doing it: in the classroom, on the athletic field, on stage, in the workplace, and in relationships, extending the performance demands to the networks of our families and circles of friends. We create the illusion that we are worthwhile and valuable because of what we are able to do and are honored for in the eyes of society and our culture. Second, we become acquisitive, basing our self-worth on what we have and on what we have acquired. Our possessions become the illusion we present to others, witnessing to and verifying that we must be really good to have succeeded in attaining a manifestly successful lifestyle, measured by such things as possessions, degrees from prestigious universities, the most highly rated auto on the market, a home in that "chic" suburban or urban setting, and a trophy partner. Slowly but surely our possessions begin to possess us, and we are like caged hamsters spinning the wheel of unending striving to possess more and more and become richer and richer.

Third, having achieved honors and obtained riches through what we have done and what we have, we can be proud. This is our crowning glory. We are content with being looked up to and smug in our looking down on others, as subtle as this posture might be. The illusion is complete: others speak highly of us and we rest, self-satisfied, above the fray and alienated from others. How hard it is to let go of such a seeming contentedness. The fortress we built becomes our prison and solitary confinement our destiny.

Which illusions are the most difficult to let go?
Carol Orsborn

I stubbornly, although understandably, can easily fall prey to the illusion that crises are somehow interruptions to the living of a spiritual life. Left to my own devices, and despite my dedication to the notion of becoming fierce with age, I have the resistant tendency to judge my level of spiritual progress by measuring the width of the rainbow on the horizon as well as counting the number of doves twittering in my heart. In other words, both when under duress and when things are going better than expected, I have the tendency to take refuge in a romanticized notion of the Sacred: that God is more readily found in serenity and peace, rather than in the scalding cauldron of complications and challenges that have been the hallmarks of so many stages of my life.

Of course I know better. In fact, I named both my digest and memoir *Fierce with Age* specifically to remind me that while God has come to me when I have been at my most serene moments, God also has come to me in my darkest hours, when I was least hopeful and most unprepared. Over time I am increasingly remembering—in both the heights and the troughs—that challenges, loss, and the many sad, bitter, and sometimes cruel faces of crises are, in fact, not impediments to the spiritual path, but the heart of it. The antidote to the illusion of God as peace is to trust that the entirety of one's journey through life is transpiring within the tender embrace of the Divine. Challenge, change, loss, and complications are not exceptions to life. But the good news is that neither are joy, peace, awe, and acceptance. The challenge is to become willing to embrace it all.

Question 13

Is there a positive purpose to keeping some of our illusions?

Carol Orsborn

Earlier in this book I wrote that mystics and seekers from many traditions yearn to transcend everyday reality to live in God's never-ending light, embraced by perfect bliss. I then intimated that this is an illusion, something that is not possible—at least not in the way that most of us tend to picture perfection.

But as I ponder the answer to this current question, I confront a profound and confounding paradox. I find myself asking, what if it is imperfection that is the illusion? What if perfection is achievable—just not yet?

What happened to me in the course of a few days that had the power to flip my thesis upside down? Simply this. We decided to sell the cottage in Los Angeles, which we had always assumed we'd retire to, in order to move to Nashville. We were drawn to live closer to family and to a better, more affordable quality of life. But another move, at this age and stage of my life, seemed daunting indeed. As I mulled the possibility, I found myself at once thrilled with the invitation while secretly clinging to the comfort of the known. I liked the way things were. Dan and I were a peaceful unit, having addressed virtually all of the tussles over the long decades of married life. I didn't need to suffer abusive bosses or nosy neighbors. I was quite content to sit alone reading a good book, finding myself saying more and more, "I don't go out at night," or "it's too much of a bother." So, did I really want to leave that all behind to take on the risk of moving back to the intimacy of family, with all its potential to not only delight and celebrate but to challenge?

Then I remembered a story from the Sufi tradition, which came to me to both awaken and instruct. There was once a Sufi whose troubles in life were no greater and no less than anyone else's. But so focused was he on achieving perfection, he decided to devote his life to finding the answer. He first went to everybody in his village, searching the compassionate faces that gathered about him for answers. They nodded and wept. Some touched his arm softly and brought him homemade soup. But still, his troubles persisted.

Realizing that there was no one in the village who could help him find the key to perfection, he set out into the unknown. Traveling alone he wandered for days, months, and then years. Everywhere he went he searched for the answer. Along the way he met many people and had many great adventures. Yet no one could help him, and so he kept on. Then one day, when he was an old man, he came to the outskirts of a village unlike any he had ever seen before. This village was surrounded by a warm mist. The homes in this village were not made of brick but of gold. As he looked around to find someone who could point him to the answers he sought, a shaft of light suddenly opened up from the very heavens, striking the front door of the grandest home in the village. He approached the large golden door and prepared to knock. But just as he raised his fist, he saw that there was a word etched into the shiny metal. "Perfection," the door read.

The man hesitated for a long moment. Then looking behind him at the long road from whence he had come—and the long road that stretched ahead—he quietly bent down to remove his shoes and tiptoed away as quickly as he could.

Like this man, I, too, suddenly realize that perfection may be achievable—but that it is a trap. To achieve perfection means the game is over—we're done. There is nothing else to achieve, no more adventures to be had. That is why traditional Japanese gardeners, after striving for as perfect a garden as possible, complete their work by throwing a handful of leaves in a corner somewhere. Likewise, American quilters always leave a flaw somewhere in their handiwork. They know, as does the Sufi, that perfection is entirely achievable—in fact, it is our destiny—but not something we need or want to achieve too soon.

We made the decision to make the move—to knowingly re-enter the fray of life with everything that entails—in order to take on the risk of becoming fully alive.

And so it is that I have come to understand not only that the notion that perfection is impossible is an illusion, but also that there is a positive purpose to maintaining this illusion. For it is only by tiptoeing away from the golden door in order to immerse ourselves in all that engagement in the world brings our way—the joy as well as the messiness—that we get to live our lives to the full.

Is there a positive purpose to keeping some of our illusions?

Bob Weber

As a psychologist one of my tasks is assisting people to face their illusions, illusions that were constructed, unconsciously, to deal with frightening and seemingly unbearable realities. The problem with such defense mechanisms is the cost they extract in diminishment of an individual's freedom and capacity to live life fully and joyfully.

There are other psychological phenomena that create illusions and appear to be defenses, but are, in fact, worth exercising because of the way they enable an individual to get on in life in the face of the frightening and unbearable. These are coping mechanisms, and, unlike defenses, they are more conscious and less automatic. They are cultivated to deal with life, to bolster a person's resiliency and competency.

Here's an example from my life. Earlier in this book I noted that in the face of my father's passing, I called upon selective inattention to make it through. Here's how the details of selective inattention actually played out. The day before I was scheduled to take my psychology licensing exam, my sister called to tell me that my father had died of a massive heart attack. The question arose: Do I take the exam tomorrow or leave immediately for my home, arriving twenty-four hours earlier than I would if I stayed and sat for the exam? If I did not take it, I would have to wait another six months before it would be given again—and, I believed, in a much less prepared and much more bereaved state because of my dad's death.

After discussing the situation and perceived realities with my wife, friends, and colleagues, I decided to sit for the exam the next day. During the exam I felt like a zombie, numb and on autopilot, using the knowledge I had packed into my brain to complete it successfully. Post-exam my wife and I raced to the airport, flew home, and joined my family in mourning and preparing for my dad's funeral. I had coped, not through the illusion of denial, but by means of a conscious use of selective inattention to the reality of Dad's death during the four hours I needed to complete the exam.

Other illusions also serve us in positive ways. The idealizations that emerge as we grow up help us to become ourselves and provide a strong support to lean on and hold on to as we develop our own capacity to navigate life—idealizations of our parents and other mentors and role models. Eventually, when we are capable of experiencing and facing their entire realities, we will de-idealize them and thereby further our own growth by fostering a more complete reality-based perception of them and of ourselves.

And let us not forget perhaps the most important illusion, the illusion that makes "the world go 'round"—Love! Miguel de Unamuno put it so well: "Love is the child of illusion!"[7] At the beginning we are seduced into loving another by the illusion of who the beloved is, whether that love is romantic or nonromantic. The disciples of Christ loved him because of their illusions about the nature of his messianic role. We choose our spouses and partners for conscious and unconscious reasons, who they really are, and who we think they are. Eventually, as we spend more time together and we get to know them more intimately, we see them as they really are, including their shortcomings and flaws.

Disillusionment sets in, and how we deal with this determines the future of the relationship. For some the disillusionment is intolerable and the relationship ends. For others, hopefully for most, the relationship begins as we grow to love the full reality of him or her, not some fantasy or illusion. This is the process of allowing disillusionment to be the beginning, not the end of a very good thing.

The resolution of love's disillusionment is beautifully illustrated in Spielberg's movie, *War Horse*. At the end of the movie, after his many failures and bad choices, Ted Narracott says to his wife, "You'll stop loving me, Rose, and I won't blame you when you do," to which she replies, "Well, I might hate you more, but I'll never love you less."[8]

Question 14

What does it mean to be free in light of the ebbing of physicality and social connection?

Bob Weber

From 1968 until 2008, for forty years, two-thirds of my life, I lived under the shadow of shame. No one who knew me, except for my wife, to whom I told my story, would have detected my shame. The things for which I felt ashamed were not even noticed by others. In fact, the circumstances out of which my shame was born were also the reasons for which people perceived me as successful, for which people respected me, and for which people had honored me at times in the past.

Nonetheless, the secret veil of shame enshrouded me even as

I moved on to further success and despite my gaining people's continued respect and regard. What was wrong with me that I could not free myself from my secret, shameful prison?

Then, in June of 2008, during my fortieth college reunion, an event occurred that began my parole from what could have been a life sentence of shameful incarceration. But first a bit of back story to that eventful moment.

Before and during my college years, I was a very successful student and athlete, garnering honors and accolades galore. In high school I graduated as the valedictorian of my class and was selected to many all-star teams in several sports, in addition to being accorded other honors. Publicly modest and unassuming, I did not realize the prideful festerings occurring beneath the surface. The sense of embarrassment I experienced in the face of these honors might have suggested this to me, if I had the psychological and spiritual insight I now enjoy.

After high school and my matriculation at a prestigious university with a promising collegiate academic and athletic career ahead of me, I was prepared for a continuation of my earlier successes, even if not consciously. But, whereas I had been the big fish in the little pond in high school, now I was one of many big fish in a big pond.

Once again my hard-working and competitive spirit undergirded my motivation for achievement and led to many successes. And again, as with my life and career in high school, this motivation was unconsciously fueled by a sense that I had not come from the same privileged circumstances as my peers, teammates, and classmates. Shame was my constant companion, and pride its ever-present mate.

All this enabled me to succeed once again and surpass many, but not all, of my more privileged and gifted classmates, academically and athletically. Academically, I was in the top 10 percent of my class, but not number one. A Rhodes Scholar state finalist, I was not selected. Although chosen as one of eleven All-American scholar athletes for the College Football Hall of Fame in 1967, I felt that my football career was a failure because of a series of injuries that dogged me and shortened playing time during my junior and senior years. Even at the last game of my senior year, when many from my hometown came to the stadium to honor me, declaring it "Bobby Weber Day," I accepted their praise sheepishly and shamefully. Even after receiving the top award given for academic and athletic success on "Senior Day" in June of 1968, I could not eradicate the shame that lingered until that day in 2008 during a reunion dinner.

All it took to change all that was a few simple memories and words: words from one of my teammates who I had determined was one of my harshest judges, perhaps the hardest worker on the team, a teammate respected by all. Who better than he to be my judge?

All he said to me was that I had gotten a raw deal and that I was the better player at my position, and that he, too, was angry about it. All I told him was that I was not kept out of the lineup for lack of respect about my abilities. I had sustained injuries that compromised my ability to perform up to the level needed by the team. The coaches had made the right decisions, and I was finally able to admit the impact of my injuries and the limitations they imposed.

I had blamed myself all those years for the failures of my body to stand up to the punishment of the game as it had done during my high school career. My body had let me down and caused me humiliation. I had to accept the fact that this was who I was: body, mind, heart, and spirit. In doing so the overshadowing shame began, and has continued, to subside, and my life is much freer and fuller.

As a result of this, hopefully, I will arrive at this sense of peace and resolution sooner when, just as injuries sidelined me on the athletic field, my aging sidelines me from my expectations of an active, uninterrupted life.

What does it mean to be free in light of the ebbing of physicality and social connection?

Carol Orsborn

For the lover of God, every moment is a moment of crisis.

ALDOUS HUXLEY

Like Bob, who supplied his definition in the introduction to this section of our guide, I felt compelled to look up the meaning of *freedom*. Enter "definition of freedom" into Google, and this is your first result: "The power or right to act, speak, or think as one wants without hindrance or restraint."

I admire the simplicity and power of this definition, but wonder how I might reconcile my lifelong urge toward increased freedom with the sober knowledge of certainty that there will, indeed, be factors that come into play that both hinder and restrain. I think of my once vigorous mother, slowly making her way down a long hallway with the help of a walker. I think of my previously affable father, lying passively in a hospital bed as he slipped into a coma.

There is some evidence that freedom may yet be possible, regardless of the ebbing away of at least a degree of physicality and social connection. Here is inspiration from the Catholic poet Paul

Claudel, who wrote in his old age: "Eighty years old . . . No eyes left, no teeth, no legs, no wind! And when all is said and done, how astonishingly well one does without them!"[9]

As Claudel instructs acceptance is a spiritual key that unlocks the door to freedom: one of the great paradoxes of aging. In the best-case scenarios, as our external faculties diminish, our internal resources—acceptance, gratitude, and faith—advance. Psychologist and interfaith minister Dr. John Robinson, in his book, *The Three Secrets of Aging,* refers to this as "coming into age." Robinson writes: "That's why we are living so much longer! We age not to get sick and die in misery but to progressively transform self and consciousness to rediscover Heaven on Earth."[10]

Facing mortality I am moved to consider that it is God's grace, and perhaps the truth that undergirds all the rest, that with the challenges, passions, and losses of aging, we are compelled to go deeper. Freedom no longer rests solely in what we recognize now were temporary constructions, leverage against the inevitable. But it is also true that I know, in my heart of hearts, that I have a long way to go.

Even before my wrestle with breast cancer, well before my confrontation with aging, I wrote about the nature of the spiritual challenges that undoubtedly lay ahead in my ironically prescient book *The Art of Resilience.* Just as back then I could not have known the exact nature, dimensions, or depth of the challenges I would face, I now look to the future, knowing there will be surprises; of this I'm sure.

Unexpected joy and unpredictable pleasure. But there are certainties, as well. There will be added pains and lessening abilities. Ultimately, there will be death. Will it be a "good" death—a gentle and loving slipping away into God's embrace? Or will it be difficult and untimely, like the deaths of some of my recent peers?

But, whichever it may be, what choice is there? As I wrote at the time, just before my breast cancer diagnosis,

> To be fully alive, we must take on the task of engaging with the circumstances of our lives—no matter how trivial, awesome, or threatening—without malice, greed, or voluntary ignorance. As we are able, we must rise to the challenges that arise moment by moment with courage and understanding. We must become brave enough to tell the truth about pain and joy, life and aging, loss and death. We must become willing to be profoundly transformed.[11]

Question 15
What still keeps you at the mercy of particular events, things, and people?

Carol Orsborn

A short while ago, while I was writing passionately about the freedom that comes from awakening to the larger, more meaningful embrace of the whole of life, Windows decided that it was the perfect time to reconfigure itself. Midsentence, the screen went blank and rebooted, before I had a chance to save a single word. The reboot took what felt to me to be ten of the longest minutes of my life, during which I had no assurances that any of the hour's work had been saved. I did not say "no worries," "at least my faith is still intact," or "that's life." No, I swore like a sailor.

Then the computer kicked back to life, and in a couple of

clicks, I discovered that it had thoughtfully saved my latest draft in some kind of emergency mode. This is perhaps a more apt symbol of where I am on the path to enlightenment—not in a permanent state of flow, but rather, raised and thrust back down again, only to be rebooted and saved, over and over, even if only in emergency mode.

Awakening is not so much a switch that goes suddenly from off to on, but a ship crossing the ocean, sometimes on serene seas, sometimes storm-tossed, as it ultimately, inexorably makes its way home.

We do make spiritual progress. Of course we continue to grow and change both as a result of learning from the things that happen to us, as well as by God's grace. But this growth is not something that occurs across the board, all at once. Rather, we may advance in one area while lagging behind in others. We may, for example, graciously accept the onset of an age-related physical disability, but be emotionally reactive to whether and how often our adult children come to visit, or vice versa.

The fact is that spiritual growth—particularly in regard to making up for missed stages—is a messy affair. As Bob and I have both noted earlier, it can appear to be far preferable and certainly easier in the moment to hang on to one's illusions and deny what is really going on. But the key to advancement is hidden in plain sight. Simply become a truth teller. *What ideas about the past do we no longer need to bring into the future? What beliefs have been imposed on us that we are hungry to leave behind? What have people said to us that we can now reject and dismiss?*

Tell the truth, feel the pain of it, and let it go. Every time we find ourselves at the mercy of old patterns, beliefs, or behaviors, we have the opportunity to make up a missed stage of our development. In the words of cultural mythologists Drs. Stanley Krippner and David Feinstein: the goal is to target old patterns of belief "that are dysfunctional, even if long held and consistently confirmed by the logic of long-standing beliefs. To the degree you are able to bring about constructive changes in such fundamental perspectives, positive shifts in your life will tend to follow."[12]

The good news is that whatever your age, it is never too late to fill in the gaps. There will come a time after doing all the hard work of surfacing, confronting, grieving, and releasing when you will know that the illusions that have held sway over you for much of your life no longer have power over you. You are learning about what it means to become free.

What still keeps you at the mercy of particular events, things, and people?
Bob Weber

After waking up and ridding yourself of illusions, you might think that there is only open highway between you and your destination. You might like to believe that the road is without traffic lights, U-turns, or detours. Just keep your foot on the gas pedal and glide on toward home. Yet we all know that this is not so.

Consider the headway you have made in your own journey, the insights, the breakthroughs, and the sighs of relief that have accompanied such moments in your life. Some endure for quite some time, yet many are more short-lived. Inevitably, you will hit a bump in the road, producing a flat tire or altering the car's alignment, disrupting your steering such that a trip to the repair shop is necessary.

So, too, in our spiritual lives. We all have events, things, and people that can still exert power over us and get us off track even if, at some point, we have awakened to the truth of how illusory they are and are able to set them in the background. When I consider my own list of the people, things, and events that have the potential to undermine my peace and centeredness, I have an array from which to choose.

And these occasions for disruption are often not the big things. There is a popular self-help book by the late Richard Carlson—another wise soul, whose passing in the prime of his life sent shock waves through literary and spiritual circles—titled *Don't Sweat the Small Stuff*. This is not bad advice, and while we should not "sweat" the small stuff, often, it is the small stuff that can be more persistently troubling and disruptive of our lives.

Each of us has a weak spot in relation to a particular event, thing, or person that creates a resonance in us sufficient to affect our tranquility, to get us agitated and vibrating. Think of how, when an opera singer's voice hits a certain pitch, it can make a wine glass vibrate, causing it to shatter into many pieces. What is the nature of the particular weak spots each of us possesses that can eventually shatter us?

A schema that helps me understand this is known popularly as the "Seven Deadly Sins." If you have some repulsion at the idea of sin, shift your thinking into a psychological context, and, instead, understand them as part and parcel of human nature, aspects of our humanity to which we all are potentially subject. A good resource for understanding this is provided by Solomon Schimmel in his book, *The Seven Deadly Sins: Jewish, Christian, and Classical Reflections on Human Nature*.

These seven aspects of our human nature are wrath, lust,

gluttony, pride, envy, greed, and sloth. When I consider my own life in light of them, I realize that I have experienced every one of them at different times and in varying degrees. I also realize that they are powerfully manifested sometimes and more subtly present at others. For example, note the smug, subtle pride inherent in a statement such as "I am proud of my humility." And, on occasion, several join together such as pride and wrath.

One of my particular "weak spots," which takes effect from time to time despite my awareness, involves just that, pride and wrath. Most often this occurs while driving in the Boston traffic, something I mentioned in an earlier section, when I spoke about my wife waking me up and encouraging me to "let it be."

As I said before Boston drivers are known for their aggressive discourteousness. Another "Boston driver" will, for example, make "a Boston left" (turn) at an intersection, forcing me to stop though I have the right of way. Given the frequency of such an occurrence, I am quite familiar with the various levels of my reaction, yet I still fall prey to the moment.

On one level my anger is justified, given the poor judgment involved in the illegal turn. Most other drivers and even a traffic judge would agree. But there is another level operating that intensifies my reaction and keeps me at the mercy of such episodes again and again. Sometimes, again something I mentioned previously, my wife will encourage me to let go of my anger, and sometimes, I am able to do so. But here's the larger truth: Other times I hold on to it, and my anger is inflamed.

Why? Because my pride was wounded. How, you might ask, was my pride injured? My wife, who knows my dynamic all too well, will kindly joke with me saying, "He wouldn't have done that if he knew it was you in this car." I was injured, in my own mind, by the fact that the other driver would never have done what he did, if he only he knew who was in the car he just cut off—Bobby Weber!

If you were to say that my thoughts are inflated and grandiose, you would be correct, for that is the nature of pride. The angry response is a cover for the injury to my pride and only exacerbates the extent to which I am at the mercy of the person and the event. At such moments, if I were still a child, I might weep for having been injured, saddened by the disregard and unkindness of others. However, my wounded pride will not admit that because such an admission would only cause more humiliation. And, so it goes, again and again, on and on!

This is one way we continue to remain at the mercy of persons, events, and things. Ask yourself what is the nature of your "weak spot"? Which of the seven deadly sins or aspects of human nature are you most subject to on an ongoing basis?

The Buddha taught that we human beings create our own suffering. The moments I just described are certainly moments of suffering, devoid of peace and joy, moments that can ruin a drive in the car or a day in a life, despite my having been awakened to it for some time and seen it for what it is. Perhaps a cartoon by Harry Bliss sheds some light on this experience. In his cartoon two Buddhist monks are seated in the lotus position, meditating. One of the monks says to the other, "Now that I'm enlightened, I have to admit: I kind of miss the suffering."

How Can We Become
More Fully Ourselves?

16. What can you accept about yourself that you previously disowned?

17. What qualities did you neglect in the first half of your life that you are now free to develop?

18. What do you especially value about yourself?

19. Who has believed in you even when you did not?

20. Do you experience yourself as having intrinsic value in the grand scheme of the universe?

THE QUESTION OF BECOMING
MORE FULLY OURSELVES

Albert Camus once wrote, "One should never indulge in useless lamentations over an inescapable state of affairs."[1] The alternative is to use the wisdom in George Santayana's observation, "There is no cure for birth and death save to enjoy the interval."[2] One of the blessings of aging is the chance to finally become, be, and enjoy the person we truly are. Enough with the "Be all that you can be!" Too much of the "You can be anything you want to be," already. Yes, we need mentors, encouragement, and models for who we might become. And hopefully, in the best-case scenario, our mentors, parents, teachers, and friends, our priests, ministers, and rabbis have wanted us to become who we really are.

However, our societal and cultural reference groups and their visions of and values for us are, unfortunately, not always geared toward us becoming and being who we really are. Even the pressure upon us to remain vibrant and youthful evades the truth of aging and thereby misses the mark. For seekers, even the wrinkles, the challenges, the very messiness of old age can take on its own special beauty, perhaps not the beauty we think of as "perfection," but certainly that most treasured of mortal attributes, "authenticity." We now have a chance to keep in mind what Eleanor Roosevelt once said, "Beautiful young people are accidents of nature, but beautiful old people are works of art."[3]

In our older age we have the chance to complete the creation of ourselves as a work of art. Then, we can stand with the likes of Michelangelo who, when asked how he actually created his sculptures, is reputed to have said that he just removed everything from the marble that was not the sculpture. And this is what we must do to become the work of art we are—deepen the integrity of the essence of our true selves. Then, perhaps, we can begin to see ourselves the way the Divine sees us.

The biblical God's vision is reflected in the following passage from the Book of Wisdom (11:24–12:1):

> *For you love all things that exist, and detest*
> *none of the things that you have made, for*
> *you would not have made anything if you*
> *had hated it.*
>
> *How would anything have endured if you*
> *had not willed it? Or how would anything*
> *not called forth by you have been preserved?*
>
> *You spare all things, for they are yours, O*
> *Lord, you who love the living.*
>
> *For your immortal spirit is in all things.*

Question 16

What can you accept about yourself that you previously disowned?

Bob Weber

As a group therapist I often see my clients disowning aspects of themselves within the dynamics of the group. It is not unusual for a whole group to disown a dimension of themselves. For example, if anger is experienced as threatening and unwanted, I will see a member or the entire group seek to off-load such feelings onto another member. Then, that individual will be seen as "the [only] angry person," who is rejected—and needed—by the group, because he serves as a repository for the undesirable feelings, like a town garbage dump.

Such a dynamic can also play out in everyday life. In a marriage relationship it is not unusual to see one partner holding one experience, such as "weakness," and the other partner another, "strength." Societally, when such a phenomenon occurs, it is "scapegoating."

We can see this every day in the denigration of a person because of his/her race, ethnicity, gender, sexual orientation, or some other characteristic. One reported origin of the word *scapegoating* is the Jewish ritual begun on Mount Shechem. The rabbi would gather the sins of the people, heap them on the back of a goat, and drive the goat into the wilderness to be devoured by the wild beasts. The community was then freed of its sins.

In psychology we call this defensive, self-protective dynamic "projective identification."[4] The first step is to split off the unwanted piece; the second step is to project that piece onto an unconsciously chosen person, the scapegoat; and, the third step that completes the dynamic is for that person (the goat) to identify with it. Of course, identifying with it, unconsciously, is usually not a problem because human nature consists of the whole spectrum of dimensions, whether manifested or not.

While the process may be less flagrant than a public scapegoating, each of us is capable of living with such a dynamic, internally and privately, which can be more painful because there is nowhere for the "unwanted" to go; it remains in us, overshadowing the "good" within us.

Two such aspects of my inner life with which I struggled were sex and aggression, what Freud called basic instinctual drives. What can you do when something that basic to your human nature and constitution is always present and must be viewed as an alien aspect, an enemy, a bad part of yourself? There is no possibility of running away from what is part of you. As Jon Kabat-Zinn wrote in titling his book, *Wherever You Go, There You Are!*

So much of what we come to see as unacceptable is determined by the people in our lives. As a child my reference groups, particularly family and church, made both sex and aggression problematic and difficult to integrate into my functioning in a normal and balanced way.

Aggression and its derivatives, anger, wrath, and competitiveness, were unwelcome. Fortunately, I had channels within which I could give such drives socially acceptable manifestations. Academic competitiveness and striving for achievement at school was one channel. The other was my participation in athletics, particularly football. In that context I could shift from the serene altar boy serving the priest at Mass to the offensive back lowering his shoulder into his opponent to gain a few more yards. I am not sure I was ever 100 percent myself at such times, but I could be the "as if" person praised by the football fans.

My sexuality was another, similar story. There was no good sex education when I was growing up. Sex education was simple: "Don't!" This was amplified by the emphasis on the sixth commandment, "Thou shalt not commit adultery," which in my experience was an umbrella commandment for everything illicitly sexual, which was everything!

This was easier said than done in the face of the raging

hormones of adolescence. While I had kind and understanding parents and priests, they, too, had discomfort with and conflicts about their sexuality. There was no one to go to, even God, whom I perceived as particularly preoccupied with the sexual dimension of our lives and its sinfulness.

Of course, this was all a manifestation of my own necessary focus on integrating my sexuality into my life. Only years later did I do so: by a willingness to look at and accept all that I am, by becoming myself in all aspects of my life, by becoming who I am. Gradually, the shame and guilt dissipated, the conflicts abated, all aspects of my sexual self were "owned," and they no longer had the power over me that they once did.

This journey all took longer than I would have liked. It taught me that I, and every person, must be patient with himself or herself and with becoming himself or herself because every individual heart is different and each has its own "timetable." This now serves others with whom I work by helping them to become more patient in the process of becoming themselves.

What can you accept about yourself that you previously disowned?
Carol Orsborn

There came upon me not long ago something I'd never anticipated: passing up the opportunity to apply for a big corporate job helping brands market to boomers. I'd always envisioned myself as an ambitious person, one who could seek and rise to any occasion. But having been previously downsized for what I vowed would be the last time, I could not bear opening myself up to the possibility of putting myself in a position where I would be underappreciated, misunderstood, or marginalized ever again. My spirit, bruises and all, was screaming at me: "You do not want to have to squeeze your feet into three-inch heels and worry about what people think about your graying hair. You don't want to tell them what they want to hear—that is based on perpetuating the stereotypes and manipulating aging boomers out of fear. You don't want to get any more feedback that what you think is most important is not of value to them."

Of course, this was not always the case. There were long periods in my life when working as a marketer carried with it immense satisfaction and rewards. But somewhere along the way I'd fallen asleep at the wheel of my life, coming to function dutifully (and even resentfully) out of habit rather than passion. In time what I ultimately came to accept about myself is that I deserved better than to believe that the only option is to push myself against my grain—judging myself by external standards. I didn't feel exaltation at the release, but something equally welcome: despite my fear at what I'd done, the faintest whisper of hope that on the other side of this, I would be free.

As I think about my last corporate job from my hard-won higher perch of age sixty-seven, I no longer wonder why it took me so long to throw off the illusion of what it means to be a success. At heart I'm a writer and teacher—not nearly as lucrative for me as the corporate job, but that which gives me true satisfaction and fulfillment. The real miracle, I now realize, is that I found it in myself to wake up at all. It took a few years to stop feeling so wobbly in the transition to my authentic life before I remembered the time, over sixty years ago, when one of my babysitters drew a picture of a face for me with a big wrinkle on the forehead and a truly sad frown. Then, magically, she flipped it upside down, and suddenly the face was grinning from ear to ear.

That's as apt a description as any of what my life is like now—at least on a good day. One moment I was frantically clutching at life, pleading with it to cough up the promised goods, thinking that if only I worked at it hard enough, I could get things to turn out right. Now I'm wandering through my life appreciating how freeing it is to no longer have to work at being myself.

Question 17

What qualities did you neglect in the first half of your life that you are now free to develop?

Carol Orsborn

The familiar life horizon has been outgrown; the old concepts, ideals, and emotional patterns no longer fit the time for the passing of a threshold is at hand.

JOSEPH CAMPBELL

Among the qualities I neglected in the first half of my life was the capacity to experience joy. I was not born that way. I clearly recall rejoicing in the mere reflection of a rainbow dancing across my bedroom wall, trying to catch the pretty colors with my outstretched hands. Every once in a while, I can still walk outdoors and be instantly transported to a time and place resplendent with the magic of early memories: a combination of the fragrance of lilacs, a certain pleasing degree of humidity, a gentle breeze and I'm back to the experience of childlike joy Bob described earlier. But sadly, just as I could not grasp the rainbow with my fingers, so, too, much of my innate capacity to experience wonder had been gradually displaced by the acquired commitment to take life seriously.

Happily, experiencing joy in the present moment is a skill that can be cultivated at any age. Not to say that this isn't a challenge for someone who learned quickly, by observing an overly cautious mother, to start each day surveying the inner and external landscape with one question in mind: What do I need to be anxious about today? Until recently, waking up had not been so much a summons to the joy of the day as it had been a call to arms. But increasingly, by God's grace, I have been taken by surprise by what is so obvious. I simply cannot sit here for twenty, thirty, or more years continuing to take life seriously—and trying to be taken seriously, as well—by grappling with shadows. I mean, really, must the legacy of concerns inherited from my well-meaning but anxious mother, long passed away, stay with me forever? Every moment of life is precious. Facing limited horizons there is no more wasting time in emotional self-indulgence masquerading as responsibility, seriousness of purpose, or even as personal growth.

This is a big turn all the way through the shadows and back into the heat of life. I want to reclaim my birthright: my name in Hebrew, which means joy, life, and light.

How am I doing? Well, I'm not doing anything grand, just lying in bed wondering whether the robins have returned and if the daffodils have bloomed yet. A fog has lifted, and in its place there is a clarity so mundane, quiet, serene, I barely noticed that something momentous had occurred. This morning, in place of waking to an onrush of anxiety, I floated awake in wonder.

Wonder is still with me as I move to my writing room, capturing my thoughts. Now I'm wrapped in a comforter crocheted by the same mother who no longer stands accused, with

Lucky curled up in my cozy lap, Molly at my feet. Ahhhhhh.

At least for today I've replaced worrying, planning, even understanding with a new subject matter for my own, private, personal self. And that is to explore and become receptive to experiencing awe and wonder. Why not? Instead of working so hard to be taken seriously, why not aspire to be an ecstatic, so on fire with love that I'm in danger of burning up?

Previously, Bob and I addressed the importance of questioning conceptions you've been holding, often unconsciously, of who you thought you were in order to reenergize your vision of who you are becoming. Like me, you may discover that there are undernourished aspects and qualities about yourself that you want to retain, expand, or deepen.

One of the gifts of longevity is that as much as we have experienced and accomplished in the past, we stand poised at the threshold of a potentially unprecedented amount of runway ahead of us: ample time to explore new ways of relating to the world. As part of this, we feel a tug at our hearts to develop qualities and potentials in ourselves we were previously too busy to attend to. We become better listeners. We can take a step back to see the bigger picture. We can stop and enjoy the moment, reminding ourselves and others what life is all about in the first place. In fact, many who have mastered certain ways of being are curious and eager to experience the exact flip side, at least for a while. What has been most interesting to me is that the flip side is different for everyone. Someone who has always been quiet and supportive of others realizes he would like to experience what it's like to be the center of attention for a change. At the same time someone who has already mastered being powerful and gathering attention to herself may crave simply to be left alone.

These new capabilities may be concrete and specific, such

as finally having the time and energy to learn to play a musical instrument or master a foreign language. But they also may be internal capabilities every bit as tangible as that which is passing away. Those of us who have worried about things in the past, may find ourselves becoming less reactive to life's circumstances. We who have been high achievers may discover an enhanced capacity to stop and smell the roses.

We've earned the right to live our lives on our own terms, whatever they may be. We are already finding ourselves less and less concerned about other people's opinions, coming to realize that what other people think of us is really none of our business. So enjoy this time of increasing freedom in your life, and don't spoil it by worrying that you are falling short of fulfilling your potential by giving yourself permission to reclaim qualities neglected in the first half of your life. Instead, give yourself the credit you deserve for being more fully yourself.

Over time most of us return to retrieve some of what we had thought to leave behind forever in order to thoughtfully meld together something authentic, original, and unshakable. This is the essence of what many of us say we want most out of life as we age: an expanded experience of freedom and an abiding sense of resolution and fulfillment. And this, too, is the very definition of not only growing old, but growing whole.

What qualities did you neglect in the first half of your life that you are now free to develop?
Bob Weber

At some point in the past, those of us who were raised in a religious household and tradition experienced what is called "religious education." In my Catholic tradition such education was called "catechism class." In class we studied the *Baltimore Catechism,* the church-approved standard manual, which consisted of sections on various topics and questions we committed to memory by rote. Then, in class, we would stand up when called on and answer the question posed by the teacher. When I was in such classes, the teachers were usually religious sisters, dressed in their ornate, formal religious garb called habits, typically black.

For example—Question One: "Who made us?" Answer: "God made us!" Question Two: "Why did God make us?" Answer: "God made us to show forth his goodness and to share with us his everlasting happiness in heaven!" The teachers praised us for our correct answers and chided as much as encouraged us when we had not studied well enough to commit them to memory, word for word. There was really no discussion of what this meant for our lives in the flesh.

I remember one section in particular, a section that cast a shadow over my life for many, many years. That was the section on sin. In it the distinction was made between sins that were "venial" (less serious) and "mortal" (very serious). If you had not confessed and been forgiven for mortal sins before you died, you were condemned to spend eternity in hell. The criteria for a mortal sin were: (1) grievous or serious matter; (2) full knowledge of the seriousness; and (3) full consent in committing the sin.

An illustration accompanied the description of these two kinds of sins. In the first, the venial sin, your soul was depicted as a bottle of white milk that had been slightly blackened and tainted by the sin. In the second, the mortal sin, the white milk was completely blackened. Needless to say, in order to be on the safe side and avoid eternal damnation, I often assumed a sin was mortal in nature, thereby causing me to live with fear and dread until I could make it to the confessional.

After confession the "milk bottle" was clean and white, and the heaviness of my dread of damnation was relieved—until I committed my next sin; then, when my scrupulosity got the better of me, leading me to believe it was more serious than it was, the dread returned, casting a shadow over my life.

My task in life was to be "a good boy." As a result there was little room for laughter and humor. I lived in a prison of rigidity and seriousness. This was reinforced by the respect and regard I received from others for being such a good boy and model child. The problem was I was not fully myself and humor was lacking. I was so concerned with avoiding the sinful humor, for example, the "dirty jokes," that I lost a free and easy sense of humor about life as a whole. I also lost connection with others, living in my own penitentiary.

Then a change came. I don't know exactly when it happened, but I know it began while I was a Jesuit and my religious education took a turn for the better. Through my introduction to Jesuit spirituality, spiritual direction to deepen my prayer life, and my theological studies to prepare for the priesthood, a sense of humor about life was born. Through the wisdom of my Jesuit mentors, I began to understand that God, too, has a sense of humor. Aphorisms like "Man plans, and God laughs" made sense to me and were not sacrilegious or blasphemous.

Last year I attended a talk by one of my current Jesuit "literary mentors," Father James Martin, SJ, a man I have never met, but whose books I have read. The talk was part of a public series at Boston College, a Jesuit University. James Martin presented material from his book entitled, *Between Heaven and Mirth: Why Joy, Humor, and Laughter Are at the Heart of the Spiritual*

Life. For those who still live the humorless life, without laughter and without mirth, I would heartily recommend his book.

For well over an hour Martin's humorous stories and jokes had us laughing so heartily that most of us, I am sure, never wanted it to end. At the same time his presentation was marked by points that elucidated the importance and seriousness of the spiritual life. He demonstrated what we all must do: find the balance between seriousness and humor, the balance between the tragedy and comedy of life.

We must also be able to contain both the joy and the sadness that are unavoidable aspects of our lives. My father-in-law, Ralph Enders, put it very well while on his deathbed, keenly aware he was coming to the end of his life. Surrounded by his children his wisdom poured out of him and he said, "How is it possible to be so sad and so happy at the same time?"

Question 18
What do you especially value about yourself?
Bob Weber

When I look back on my childhood, my adolescence, and my young adulthood, I now see how trapped I was in my own skin, though I had no idea this was the case. And when I realize what I valued about myself and what others valued about me, I understand the causes of my imprisonment.

Through my late twenties I focused on what others valued about me and my own internalization of their values. While this gave me life in many ways, in other ways I was a dead man. By contrast, when I think of what I now value about myself, I feel alive.

As I think of that which I value about myself, a number of aspects come to mind. Although I am inclined to rank order them, I prefer to view each one as of equal importance, each part interacting with the others to create the person I am.

A short list begins with my generosity to friends and others, my sense of humor, my willingness to face the bad and unpleasant aspects of myself, while not dismissing the good in me that balances the whole of me. It includes my capacity to cry and weep, whether out of sadness or joy, when I am so moved, and my freedom to laugh from the belly about the comedy that is sometimes life itself. As important is my growing ability to laugh at myself, to not take myself so seriously, and to laugh with others, not at others.

My lifelong spiritual yearnings loom large as well. From the peaceful quiet of the church at dawn in a half-light, to the experience of existential dread and the hope of a safe harbor, my ongoing spiritual odyssey remains central to my life.

Then there are my tender and loving ways with others that I value and treasure. Over the years I have become freer to manifest and give expression to both without shame, without the sense I am not manly enough when I do so. As I have become more true to myself, the falseness in me diminishes. The false self, the more macho male, the fruit of cultural learning for us males grows weaker and less predominant.

When I asked my wife what it is she loves about me and what she thinks others love about me, I found a congruence between what others value and what I value. This congruence grows the more I am able to be true to myself and to manifest what I value about myself in my life with others.

Early on in my relationship with my wife of thirty-five years, I found myself struggling to say the words "I love you," despite my certain awareness that I did. Now the words just flow out when I know and appreciate how much I do love her. At the same time this experience of my loving self has increased an awareness of my vulnerability, for love is a risky business that requires not just submission to the feelings, but surrender to them.

These days, as my awareness of my own aging grows, I sense I am being brought to appreciate and value even more my vulnerability and my capacity to surrender that has evolved through the years and through my relationships. Slowly and sometimes not so gradually, the changes occurring in me as a result of aging threaten to swamp me with dread. At such times I have begun to hope that my vulnerability and the invitation to surrender, more and more, is offering me a spiritual path to greater fullness of life, now and in the future.

What do you especially value about yourself?
Carol Orsborn

Moving beyond midlife brings to us the opportunity to question old conceptions of who we are and to invite new ways of being into our lives. This may sound easier to do than it really is. When I was on the on-ramp to my sixties, I became hyperfocused on those qualities and characteristics I hoped to leave behind. Answering a question about what I especially value about myself would have sent me into a toxic mix of introspection, regret, and self-pity. In the words of my eighty-something mentor, writer and wise woman Connie Goldman: "Sometimes, it seems like only the good parts have dropped away, and the disliked parts, such as worrying, judgments, and the like are the only parts that remain." But happily, Connie goes on. "The thing is: the falling away—this is growth, too."[5]

Taking courage from Connie, I will say that the one thing I especially and consistently value about myself, the one thing that never seems to have dropped away—at least for long—is my urge toward becoming increasingly whole. I am a seeker to the very bottom of my soul, paying heed to the still, quiet voice that alternately issues from head, heart, and gut, and that holds the promise of unity with the Divine. It is as if I once experienced the sublime wholeness of complete and total self-acceptance. More than acceptance: a thoughtless merging with the unity of the Universe, which I experienced, recognized, and remember as pure love. From this perspective I view everything else as a means to overcoming the obstacles that will ultimately lead me back to this unity. And aging, with all its challenges and opportunities, efficiently serves to quicken the pace. This is why, as I pass the threshold from midlife to older age, I have increasingly come to embrace aging not as the culmination of my spiritual growth, but in many ways, as the beginning. In fact, I would have to say that the quality I most appreciate about myself—and that others appreciate most about me as well—is my acute awareness of aging as a mystical path.

While writing my memoir *Fierce with Age: Chasing God and Squirrels in Brooklyn,* I reread the work of Sam Keen, whose *Hymns to an Unknown God* has been on my bookshelf for years. When I'd purchased the newly published book fifteen years previously, Sam had been in his sixties. I recalled having liked the book a lot the first time through, viewing Sam as a sage and worldly elder. But this time, as I read the book, grown-up to grown-up, I felt both chastened and inspired by his spiritual maturity.

Sharing passages of the book with a friend who was

going through a rough patch herself, I found the key to self-acceptance:

> Much of the turmoil of my life has come from struggling to actualize some fantasy or realize an ideal of self that is unfitting. I would like to be happy-go-lucky, leisurely, of lighter spirit. I fool myself into wishing I were somebody totally different from who I actually am. I am unhappy because I am burdened by the demon of philosophy, cursed always to be asking "why," an obsessive worker at the meaning game. But then in an instant, my perspectives shift, and I accept what before was problematic. I view my history, my parents, my body type, my strange appetite for asking questions, and my unsettled and unsettling mind as my destiny. What was a wound is transformed into a gift. In that moment I know that my ultimate freedom lies in surrendering to this strange being who bears the name Sam Keen.[6]

It has taken me a long time to get to the place where I can say that I am finding freedom in surrendering to this strange being who bears the name Carol Orsborn. The wound has, indeed, been transformed into a gift.

Question 19
Who has believed in you even when you did not?
Carol Orsborn

I have been blessed with a great marriage. I have dedicated many of my twenty plus books to my husband, Dan, but because both Dan and I prefer to keep certain aspects private, I have restricted him to bit parts and guest appearances in the published narratives of my life. But this question, after all these thousands of pages, begs that I break through the family protocol.

Dan and I have been together since we were twenty-one. That's a lot of years and a lot of growing through life side by side. I have to admit that when we first met, I was certainly in need of saving. My transit from childhood to young adulthood was wild, sometimes misguided, and at the same time passionate. These were qualities that over the decades would be subtly, persistently, and sometimes traumatically crafted into fierce independence and vital ambition. But the biggest transformation of all was from believing myself to be essentially unlovable, to somebody who knows and trusts that she is deeply, unconditionally beloved.

A good marriage, or friendship, or any manner of relationship, where mistakes are allowed to fall away and love persists, is the training ground for mystical union. Visiting the grave of an old friend, I was deeply moved by the carving on the headstone, a quote from the Song of Solomon: "I am my Beloved's, and my Beloved is mine." Theologians read this as a metaphor for unity with the Divine. And so it is that my marriage to Dan has more often than not allowed me glimpses into what I'd always hoped was the case: that this is, indeed, a loving universe.

Hope, however, is not the same as belief. Belief grew slowly, day after day, spat after spat, transgression after transgression. Of course, our love grew through good times as well as bad. But it wasn't until I was able to let the entirety of my existence unfold within the embrace of a blessed union that I truly came to understand what the key building blocks of a loving universe would consist of: qualities like compassion, generosity, and forgiveness.

One of my earliest memories of Dan's and my relationship—and the moment I knew that I would marry this man—was after one of those many times earlier in life when I did something stupid or selfish (happily, I can't remember the exact specifics after all these years) at Dan's expense. I immediately felt remorse and regret, but braced myself for what prior to Dan had been the norm. I would be frozen out, disproportionately berated, or forced to witness the guilt of having inflicted a mortal wound on another. But none of these occurred. Dan may have told me in firm but neutral language what he had witnessed in my behavior (if not then, certainly many times since, as Dan is very able to draw boundaries and tell the truth about what he is experiencing). But here was the miracle: As I cowered in the aftermath of the exchange, attempting yet another in a long string of apologies, Dan stopped me short. "What are you talking about?" he asked without guile. "I don't remember anything." And with a smile and an embrace, the incident that had transpired was over. Just like that. A clean slate.

Dan always believed in the best of me—rather than the worst. And over the years, consistently privileging his belief in my capacity to be my best possible self, I gradually and finally came to believe it as well.

Who has believed in you even when you did not?
Bob Weber

After ten years as a member of the Jesuit religious community, a delay of ordination, a leave of absence, and several years of therapy, spiritual direction, and prayer, I decided to leave the Jesuit community in which I had lived a vowed life of poverty, chastity, and obedience, a community that I had grown to love and respect. Bob, my Jesuit superior, the man in charge of men in preparation for ordination at the time, was very patient with me during the roller coaster ride I underwent in coming to my decision. He gave me the room I needed to discern that this was what I needed to do in order to continue becoming myself.

Jesuits establish strong bonds of filial affection and loyalty, making it difficult not only for a man who decides to leave the community, but for those who are left. (I lost a number of Jesuit friends who resented my exit.) Nonetheless, Bob gave me all the room I needed without exerting any pressure to remain.

Bob not only believed in the discernment process but he also believed in me, my integrity, and my decision-making process, even as I struggled through doubt, spiritual darkness, and depression on the way to my decision. To this day he remains my friend, spiritual director, and witness to my continued seeking to grow more and more into myself.

Before Bob's direction I had worked with Joe, a man I deeply admired, respected, and loved. It was Joe's work with me that actually enabled me to get to the decision to take a leave of absence and delay ordination; however, Joe was not privy to the final period of my discernment process when I finalized plans to leave the community and request release from my vows.

Despite feeling uneasy about telling Joe that I was leaving, I arranged an appointment and went to see him. After our initial greeting and a brief period of chitchat, I got right to the reason for my visit and told him I was leaving. Immediately, he began to ask me if I had considered this and that and if I had thoroughly thought and prayed through my process. Suddenly, I felt the kind of pressure I experienced growing up, though now I was more much connected to my true self and much more aware of the pressure I had felt as a kid, which was unconsciously affecting my life choices.

I stopped Joe in his tracks and told him I had done everything he was suggesting. My mind and heart were settled, and I was ready to leave despite my fears and anxieties about the unknown path that was ahead of me. I made it clear I had not come to seek further direction; I had come to say goodbye as a fellow Jesuit and to let him know how much affection, love, and gratitude I had for him because of the part he played in my growing into a man. We hugged and wept.

Although my family was aware of my leave of absence from the Jesuits, they were neither part of, nor intimate with my internal deliberations nor struggles. The day came when I was ready to tell them that my mind and heart were made up, and I was ready to leave. As I mentioned earlier, my father, whose desire for me to be a priest and whose wishes for me I was fulfilling, had the strongest reaction. He was disappointed and angry. He made it known, pointing out things about me that had the potential to stir up guilt and shame, but I stood my ground and stood up to him.

For a lengthy period of time, several years I recall, there was a tension and distance between us. It did not matter. At the time, between the ages of twenty-eight and thirty-two, I was traversing what Daniel Levinson, a Yale psychology professor and author of *The Seasons of a Man's Life*, called the "boom years."[7] "Boom" is an acronym for "becoming one's own man." The word boom also represents the explosiveness of what happens for the man in transition and for those with whom he is close, as it did for me, with Joe, and with my father.

Several years later, while I was completing graduate school, marrying Pamela, and settling my life in ways far different than

I or my father had ever imagined, my father and I spoke more openly. After having grappled with his own anger and disappointment over my decision, he came through, as he always had, as a father who loved me, only now in a much more mature way. He loved me for becoming myself. He put it simply, "All I really ever wanted for you was your happiness."

Despite whatever hopes, doubts, fears, or angers these three men—Bob, Joe, and my father, Lou—felt for and toward me, the bottom line, as I discovered, was that they loved me. And their love encouraged and sustained me, still sustains me, to never cease becoming myself.

Question 20

Do you experience yourself as having intrinsic value in the grand scheme of the universe?

Bob Weber

In my therapeutic group work with patients, I have encountered many who, despite what other group members or I say, cannot believe that they are as beloved as they have become in our eyes; despite all things about them being considered, their good qualities, bad habits, and aspects of character that they have revealed. The protests are usually simple and direct; for example, to me, the group leader, they say, "You get paid to say such things." To other group members they say, "If you really, really knew me, you would not be able to say such a thing about me." Typically, such a response is crafted while in the face of deeply felt shame that resides within them, hidden from public scrutiny, hidden from themselves.

Such moments also stir up in me questions about my own goodness and value. I, too, am aware of the many shameful dimensions of myself that are my legacy as a man and a human being. As I mentioned earlier I have an issue getting angry with bad drivers. Just yesterday, while driving with my wife, we both delighted in appreciating, for the first time, the deeply spiritual dimension of one of Tony Bennett's signature songs, "If I Ruled the World." I was transported into a deeply peaceful, joyful, and spiritual state of being. The next moment, with a large pickup truck tailgating us, my wife shifted lanes to allow him to pass, and I swore at the driver as he left us in his dust.

If neither my patients nor I can escape the ugly realities of ourselves, how can we trust and believe that we are valued and loved by others? Perhaps we can fool others by hiding the truths about ourselves, truths that are only unwittingly disclosed and revealed. However, if we believe in a God, how can we imagine that God values us and loves us, given we are known through and through by such a being? Can we ever expect such a God would say to us, "You are my beloved son [or daughter] in whom I am well-pleased?" Consider Psalm 139: 1–14.

> *O Lord, you have searched me and known me. 2 You know when I sit down and when I rise up; you discern my thoughts from far away. 3 You search out my path and my lying down, and are acquainted with all my ways. 4 Even before a word is on my tongue, O Lord, you know it completely. 5 You hem me in, behind and before, and lay your hand upon me. 6 Such knowledge is too wonderful for me; it is so high that I cannot attain it. 7 Where can I go from your spirit? Or where can I flee from your presence? 8 If I ascend to heaven, you are there; if I make my bed in Sheol, you are there. 9 If I take the wings of the morning and settle at the farthest limits of the sea, 10 even there your hand shall lead me, and your right hand*

shall hold me fast. 11 *If I say, "Surely the darkness shall cover me, and the light around me become night,"* 12 *even the darkness is not dark to you; the night is as bright as the day, for darkness is as light to you.* 13 *For it was you who formed my inward parts; you knit me together in my mother's womb.* 14 *I praise you, for I am fearfully and wonderfully made. Wonderful are your works; that I know very well.*

What is helping me to appreciate that I am valuable in the eyes of God, all of my being notwithstanding? The animals in my life! "The animals in my life?" you think to yourself! This statement coming from a psychologist! How do animals help to answer such a profound question? Two recent experiences with animals drove home the point.

For the past several years my wife was hounding me about getting another dog. Coco, a chocolate Labrador retriever, was our beloved pet for twelve years, from the age of 3½ years, when we acquired him from Lab Rescue, until we had to put him down at age 15½ years, when an inoperable tumor hemorrhaged the day before our two-week summer vacation. After his death we spent the first week of our vacation sobbing daily for our beloved companion. Part of me was reluctant to get another pet, to avoid the loss that accompanies such an attachment. I did not want to go through such grief once again.

Knowing how much it meant to my wife, I reluctantly acquiesced and we received Rosie, a six-month-old yellow Lab, from a breeder in Rangeley, Maine on December 30, 2012. In the early days, and weeks, and months that followed, I resisted every impulse to form an attachment with Rosie. Nonetheless, gradually, she wore me down and I began to love her and appreciate her presence in my life. In the process I learned something both about my love for God and God's love and appreciation for me. Another scriptural passage came to my mind and heart that embellished my experience with Rosie and my relationship with God.

In Matthew's Gospel (15:21–28) a Canaanite woman approaches Jesus, requesting help for her demon-possessed daughter. Initially both his disciples and he rebuff her very unkindly, in a way that seems so out of character for Jesus, who says, "I was sent only to the lost sheep of the house of Israel. . . . It is not right to take the food of the children and throw it to the dogs." Nonetheless, the woman persists, and answers him with the retort "even the dogs eat the scraps that fall from the table of their masters."

I can imagine myself on both sides of this interaction between the Canaanite woman and Jesus. In empathy with the woman, my plight necessitates that I be importunate because there is too much at stake: the well-being of a daughter, whom I love as much, even more than I love myself. I am willing to humble myself and grovel to get what I want, the kindness and compassion of Jesus.

As Jesus I am stretched to grow in appreciation and valuation of this Canaanite woman—undervalued in the culture for being both a woman and a foreigner. This story tells about the true nature of God, as a being that values not just the in-crowd, but also the out-crowd pariahs. The woman wins over Jesus and enjoys his love and compassion for both her and her daughter.

Through my experience with Rosie I am growing more convinced of the depth of God's love for us humble creatures, men, women, and animals alike. I grow more convinced every day of the value, based on love, that is ours in the being of God. Every time we experience the love for one of God's creatures, human or nonhuman, we apprehend the nature of God's love of us and the value placed on our being-ness.

Do you experience yourself as having intrinsic value in the grand scheme of the universe?

Carol Orsborn

One of the challenges of aging is reviewing even one's noblest aspirations, and finding them wanting. From as early as I can remember, I wanted God to see me as valuable. As I review my progress it is so easy to feel disappointed, bitter even, that not only I, but so many of our generation have expended so much energy trying to change the world—and come up short. We wanted to move things forward by a mile, and instead, moved things maybe an inch. In some ways things have gone "bass ackwards" and it is hard to watch our peers and our children struggle with issues we'd hoped to have fixed for good. Changing the world turned out to be a taller order than we thought. So, given the failure of my efforts to do God's work, do I believe that God yet sees me as valuable?

Meaning and purpose, as it turns out, do not always come passively, like the time I was four and felt God in a beam of sunlight for the first time. I recognized, noted, memorized the moment to be called up for the rest of my life: a touchstone as tangible as the warmth hitting the open palm of my hand. Sometimes certainty comes as effortlessly as the beam of sun in the palm of a hand. But sometimes certainty is something we wrestle for, like Jacob struggling through the long night with a dark angel on the banks of the Jabbok, winning God's blessing, but not without injury. I'm not willing to give up hope, even yet. But holding faith, not only for myself but also for so many others, is not always a joy. It is often a struggle. In the struggle I still feel the urge to step in, to extoll, solve, save. But sadly, I confront my limitations. I can't answer for God. That was never my place. I know that now, as I have to make tough choices, based on increasingly limited resources and a life that is running out of runway.

What convinces me that God yet finds me valuable? I am taking solace from a talk by James Finley, the former Trappist monk, who was schooled by Thomas Merton. In a talk about Meister Eckhart, Finley addressed the question of winning that place of unity of God: the sense that we have done, been, and are enough, that we are valued. At talk's end he was asked the question: "Why can't we live in that place of merger all the time?" Paraphrasing Finley's reply: "What's your hurry? You'll get there soon enough when you die." "But I want more of it now!" the questioner replied. Finley thought a moment, then instructed: "You have fallen short of fulfilling your aspirations? That abandonment, that fear, that sadness—it will never go away. But it can be transformed. How? Through God's compassion. You stop trying to get rid of the pain, stop trying to run away from it, outgrow it, master it and rather accept it, deepen it, and suddenly you understand, no, more, you experience that all of your life—the pain, the disappointment, and the joy, as well—they are all within God's tender embrace."[8]

What if the only true experience of profound happiness—the certainty that God sees one as valuable—comes when we accept the pain will always be there? Finley ended with a story that provides both added illumination and hope. Imagine you live in a village, and all your life you aspire to get to the top of the mountain, where you are certain there is the loving presence of God. For years you struggle up the mountain toward your destination and, at long last, you are just yards away. Then, uninvited, you hear a cry coming from the valley below. Somebody is sobbing. What should you do? If you are in touch with your heart, you turn around and go back down the mountain to attend to the crying. You walk through the village, following the sobs, and are led to the front door of your very house. You open the door and there in the corner is a young child. You look more closely: it is not just any young child; it is you. You go to your young self to provide comfort, your heart bursting with compassion, as the young child gratefully nestles in your arms. And then, suddenly transported, you look up, and you are both at the top of the mountain.[9]

What Is the Value of Aging to Society?

21. Can withdrawal from the mainstream, by choice or circumstances, have value?

22. What is the dynamic tension between accepting marginalization and fighting against it?

23. Is there a spiritually/psychologically healthy response to those times when you feel disconnected from the Sacred?

24. What value, if any, do those who have suffered in their aging such things as cognitive impairment and physical pain hold for us?

25. How can spiritual maturity equip us to face our own unknowns?

THE QUESTION OF THE VALUE OF AGING

We began this part of our book with the Question of Spiritual Maturity. Over the course of these past twenty questions, you were guided to take a deeper look at not only where you were coming from in regard to your attitudes and beliefs about aging, but the progress you've made in the embrace of a fuller, richer vision of the possibilities.

By now, you know that you are not alone. An increasing number of individuals in our generation are discovering the potential inherent in aging to provide a culmination to the spiritual path we have been walking most of our lives. This does not mean it's easy: waking up from illusion to embrace both the shadow and light of aging and mortality is hard work. As Rick Moody put it so eloquently in his article "Conscious Aging: A New Level of Growth in Later Life": "Conscious Aging—the holistic line of development—is not an easy path nor is Conscious Aging likely to appeal to a majority of those entering old age."[1]

So why embark on this path in the first place? What is the value of aging, to ourselves and to society? Let's begin with a story about the value of aging to society. In the 1950s anthropologist Margaret Mead delivered a memorable lecture that has relevance to our consideration. Her discussion centered on the role of postmenopausal red-tailed deer in their herd. From the outside these old does appeared to have no value. Their male counterparts, charged with protection of the herd, had all been killed off over the years. It would be natural to think of the elderly who remained as burdens to the herd. But this was not the case.

Mead goes on: "In time of drought, these old does could remember where once, long ago, under similar circumstances, water sources had been found. When spring came late, they recalled sunny slopes where the snows melted early. They knew how to find shelter, places where blizzards could be waited out. Under such circumstances, they took over the leadership of the herd."[2]

Margaret's story goes straight to the heart of the question at hand, standing in stark contrast to contemporary Western society: a culture that still tends to think of aging as a problem, marginalizing, ignoring, and even reviling the elderly. But just as the old does knew where to find sunlight, we who are growing old have knowledge and wisdom to share with others, inner reserves of resources upon which to call that are often dismissed too readily by those who would benefit the most.

Not all of what we have to contribute is internal, either. Many of us are crossing the transom beyond midlife with the energy and desire to give back. We feel the pull of legacy, the promise of purpose and, as we referenced earlier, what Erik Erikson called the passion for generativity.[3] Many of us have the time and resources to volunteer, to mentor, and to contribute. Spiritual maturity carries with it the organic urge to make a difference: to do our utmost for as long as possible.

But here, too, is the paradox of age. For even as we respond to the yearning to utilize our skills and abilities to the full for the greater good, we feel a tug at our hearts to develop qualities and potentials in ourselves too long neglected. Sometimes by choice, sometimes by circumstances, we come to realize how much of our sense of mastery over our fates had always been limited. Embracing aging with humility, acceptance, and surrender, we enter, at last, the realm of the mystic, finding ourselves walking a path that has inherent value of its own.

While walking aging as a spiritual path is deeply personal, it bears implications for society at large. According to Moody this deeper embrace of the whole of life has emerged as a new cultural ideal at a specific moment in history representing "a genuinely new stage and level of psychological functioning . . . The evolution of psychology toward a deeper view of the human person can now join with the societal transformation of institutions to create new opportunities for positive development in later life."[4]

As Moody teaches conscious aging is not for everybody. But for those of us who have embarked on aging as a spiritual path, it is an exciting time, indeed, to be growing old.

Question 21

Can withdrawal from the mainstream, by choice or circumstances, have value?

Carol Orsborn

Thomas Merton devoted much of his adult life to addressing the answer to this question. While Merton himself was torn between his own passion for contemplative living and the growing demands upon him through the enthusiastic response with which his writing was met, he was clear about the value of withdrawal. In observing the Poor Brothers of God, fellow monks who had chosen to withdraw from society, he writes: "In their cells, they tasted within them the secret glory, the hidden manna, the infinite strength of the Presence of God . . . You felt that the best of them were the simplest, the most unassuming, the ones who fell in with the common norm without fuss and without special display. They attracted no attention to themselves. They just did what they were told. But they were always the happiest ones, the most at peace."[5]

It doesn't occur to most of us that the individual apparently "doing nothing" may be having a transcendent experience. Recall my earlier example of the elderly woman sitting alone on a park bench. If we see her at all, what we want most for this person is for her to have a makeover and join a gym. But what a waste of the human potential this is, to only define successful aging— or life, for that matter—in youth-centric terms of productivity, activity, and vigor. I am reminded here of an apocryphal story from the Hindu tradition about Alexander the Great. As the story goes Alexander was leading his troops through India when he spotted a saint sitting serenely on the banks of the river.

"I wish I could just be sitting there as you are, enjoying the sun," Alexander said.

"Where are you going?" the saint replied.

"I'm going to fight one more battle and then I will return to sit beside you." The saint looked deeply into Alexander's eyes and said:

"If what you really want in the end is to sit here with me by the river, why don't you just do it now?"

Mystics from virtually all spiritual and religious traditions have discovered the same thing: that it is times like these that strip away addiction to busyness, and the illusion of fulfillment it falsely promises. Detached from the status quo, we have the opportunity to transform and transcend, addressing the larger questions of life, about meaning and purpose, as we go.

Describing the monastic perspective, Thomas Merton put it this way: "The logic of the Cistercian life was, then, the complete opposite of the logic of the world, in which men put themselves forward, so that the most excellent is the one who stands out, the one who is eminent above the rest, who attracts attention . . . The logic of worldly success rests on a fallacy: the strange error that our perfection depends on the thoughts and opinions—and applause of other men!"[6]

Alexander was too busy, too goal-driven to pay heed to the saint's sage advice. And so it is, too, that so many of us rush through the many decades of our lives consumed with logistics, responding to emergencies, and fulfilling goals. Some of us encounter challenges earlier in life that slow us down, such as serious illness, divorce, or in some cases, recognition that there's quite simply got to be more to life than just scurrying around. This is the lesson that aging makes more and more accessible to us, as the losses associated with the aging process naturally slow us down. In fact, those of us who embrace rather than deny the shadow side of aging can discover something both novel and transformational. We don't need to do anything more to help us understand the transitory nature of life. We are living it.

Can withdrawal from the mainstream, by choice or circumstances, have value?

Bob Weber

Recently, I found and purchased a book that became number one on my list of books to read, a book by Thomas and Cindy Senior entitled *The Joys of Getting Older*. First I read the testimonials on the front and back covers such as "A straightforward, clear-cut-how-to-book for putting a spark (or two!) back into your life." Another by Yule Biyung read "It truly describes the magical beauty to be found in the twilight years."[7] Then I opened the book and found a sheaf of empty, white pages! Apparently there is NOTHING TO SAY about "the joys of getting older." There is nothing joyful about aging.

Peggy Lee and the refrain from her signature song came to mind, "Is That All There Is?" "Is that all there is, my friend? Then let's keep dancing and break out the booze."[8] Is there no joy, no value in aging? Is there a legitimate basis for ageism and good reasons for marginalizing us older folks, us baby boomers? Should we, like the aging elephant, take ourselves off to the graveyard? Do we absorb society's assessment of us, its beliefs, attitudes, norms, and values about aging, and devalue ourselves and our senescence? Then, do we consign ourselves to the valueless junk heap?

Or do we view aging from a different vantage point? Do we stand with Wendy Lustbader and say with her, as her book title does, *Life Gets Better: The Unexpected Pleasures of Getting Older*. Wendy is an experienced geriatric social worker in Seattle, Washington. She takes off the lenses of ageism and invites us to see aging in a different light, as she herself has seen it and as her many clients have helped her to see it, while not denying the fear and dreaded realities of aging. Wendy invites us to up-value the experience of aging and reenvision the integration of our life's experiences, the deepening of our wisdom, and the sense of blessing, peace, and joy that results.[9]

What if we baby boomers were to embrace our aging and accept and reframe the marginalization imposed on us by society? One image I have found very useful was provided by my colleague and friend, Dr. Jane Marie Thibault, a gerontology professor emerita, in her paper, "Aging as a Natural Monastery," that appeared in *Aging & Spirituality,* the newsletter of the American Society on Aging's Forum on Religion, Spirituality and Aging.

For many years Dr. Thibault has worked as a spiritual director for the monks of the Trappist Abbey of Gethsemani in Kentucky, the monastery that was, until his death in 1968, the home of Thomas Merton. Echoing Merton, Thibault explains that the monk withdraws from and embraces the marginal position relative to society and culture. From that vantage point the monk, through prayer and other spiritual practices, opens himself or herself up to a more transcendent reality that sets day-to-day life in a broader perspective and gives it coherence. This perspective allows for greater awareness of self and other and often shines a healthy and critical perspective on the inherent and unquestioned beliefs, attitudes, norms, and values that permeate our society and ourselves.[10]

In the process of embracing rather than rejecting such a marginal position, a monk perceives the shallowness of such beliefs, and gradually becomes more who he truly is. A number of truths about life and living pervaded Merton's writings through the years. One of the most prominent was the contrast between our true and false selves. Recall an earlier quote from Merton's book, *No Man is an Island,* "Every man has a vocation to be someone; but he must understand clearly that in order to fulfill this vocation he can only be one person: himself."[11] Our societal and cultural beliefs, attitudes, norms, and values create a false sense of identity, a false self, living a life built on illusions that our worth is based on the mainstream values of economic success and advantage, social privilege and status, and name recognition—the things I can do, the things I have, and the esteem in which I am held by others who subscribe to the same values.

The monk and the aging person, that is, all of us, have the choice to disengage from what we hold on to "for dear life" and what holds on to us, keeping us from living our dear lives. Earlier Carol cited the work of James Finley. One of Merton's novices, James Finley, decided that being a Trappist monk was not his vocation and left the monastery after six years. Nonetheless, he continues to be monastic outside the cloister, working to pass on the message he internalized while at Gethsemani.

In his book, *Merton's Palace of Nowhere: A Search for God through Awareness of the True Self,* Finley gives us another way to state Thibault's notion of "aging as a natural monastery," inviting us to embrace the marginal position by free choice:

> The Contemplative, the prophet, is thus for Merton the marginal person ... He does not belong to an establishment. He is a marginal person who withdraws deliberately to the margins of society with a view to deepening fundamental human experience. ... The marginal person, the monk, the displaced person, the prisoner, [and I would add "the aging" to Finley's list] all these people live in the presence of death, which calls into question the meaning of life.[12]

Question 22
What is the dynamic tension between accepting marginalization and fighting against it?
Bob Weber

Athletic coaches often say that your sports experience and training is preparing you for life. Little did I understand what that platitude meant at the time of my high school and college careers in sports. Little did I realize how it would apply to getting older, approaching the end of life, and making sense of the experiences that would accompany my aging.

Earlier I alluded to the injuries I experienced during my career in sports and how they impacted my self-esteem. I recall one period in particular. In the late summer of 1966, I participated in a three-week preseason football camp in Blairstown, New Jersey, in preparation for the upcoming Princeton University season. It was my junior year, and I was slotted as the number one tailback for our single-wing formation, a position that required three skills: running, passing, and kicking. All summer long I had worked out diligently and entered camp in excellent physical shape, ready to assume my responsibilities and take on a pivotal role for the team.

Several days into camp, during wind sprints, which always concluded our morning and afternoon sessions, I pulled a hamstring muscle and ended up lame. This pull threw my preparation off, interfered with camp, and dogged me for the season. All of a sudden my potential role was jeopardized by injury, which was further exacerbated by a shoulder injury midway through the season. Never before in my high school or early college years had I been so plagued by injuries.

The 1966 team went on to a successful season, winning the Ivy League title while I watched from the sidelines, marginalized by injury, and relegated to the bench except for occasional time on the field. The man who had been my understudy, a sophomore, assumed the tailback's role, starred, and played an instrumental role in the team's success.

As a result I felt humiliated and, though I did not know it, depressed, throughout my junior year because a primary basis for my identity and worth was stripped from me by the failure of my body on the playing field. The depression ate into my academic performance as well, and my grades slipped from what they had been my first two years. I reached the low point of my college years.

In retrospect I consider this period a time of "crisis," though, at the time, I did not think in those terms. As I wrote earlier, the word *crisis* has its roots in the Greek language, meaning "a time of decision," "a time of judgment," and "an opportunity." At twenty I did not fathom the possibilities inherent in the experiences I was going through. All I saw was the darkness and the pain caused by the failure of my body, the loss of my role, and the sidelining marginalization that resulted. No longer a BMOC, a "big man on campus," I felt like the forgotten man on campus.

So, what has that marginalization been teaching me that I did not learn then but which I am learning now?

Having turned sixty-nine years of age, I am verging on a much more potentially profound marginalization due to aging and ageism than being sidelined during a game. What can you and I learn from my experience in the face of the marginalization aging is likely to bring us? Should our sidelining by aging be fought or accepted? What does either one cost us? What does either one get us? How can the tension of the choice, the decision(s) we face, serve us?

I was graced with the realization that I was more than just a football player and that I had always been more than that, though my identity and worth were built on that role and identity for many years. With the end of my football career, I had the chance to be more of who I was.

Now, you and I, as we face marginalization due to aging and ageism, face the crisis of getting older and have a choice to become and be more who we are, living from the inside out rather than the outside in. We do not need to fight or accept marginalization. We do need to reenvision ourselves in terms that transcend the limits of sociocultural values in which we are embedded and about which we are unconscious. Aging is a wake-up call, a chance to wake up as I did at the end of my last football season, and an opportunity to discover, even more, who I really am, deep inside.

What is the dynamic tension between accepting marginalization and fighting against it?

Carol Orsborn

When Bob and I began the conversation in the stairwell that ultimately birthed this book, I was torn between two voices in my heart vying for my attention. One told me that as a lifelong writer, I was obligated to push myself and others in order to continue to play some kind of public role. The other voice, equally loud, was urging me to withdraw from the worlds of ambition and productivity in pursuit of the contemplative life, luring me inward with the tantalizing intuition that there could be inherent value in not only accepting but proactively pursuing marginalization from the mainstream. Which voice would emerge triumphant—or could there be a third option luring me toward the reconciliation I seek?

I now realize that the fact that I could even entertain this question with any degree of seriousness was a spiritual opportunity. Clearly, I was yearning to make a clean break from old, exhausting habits and ways of relating to the world. Among the gifts of aging is the time and opportunity to develop aspects of ourselves that were underdeveloped during the busy years that comprised the hard work of prior life stages.

Earlier I wrote about the decision to move from Los Angeles to Nashville, to live closer to our grand family. But that was only part of the draw. That decision had been divinely affirmed when during the course of writing this book we found and then purchased an old stone cottage on the Cumberland River, just fifteen minutes from the family, in nearby Madison. From the moment we'd first spotted the house, I had pictured myself sitting on the riverbank in a state of bliss. In reality several months came and went before I actually took a seat by the bank for anything other than entertaining friends with barbecue. All that time, the river was alternately flirting and scolding me as I rushed about the house, too preoccupied with the aftermath of the move, my suddenly extended family dynamics, and questions about my future as a writer to stop and sit. And while it was always fun, beautiful, or exciting to look at, the river had inspired nothing close to bliss. But as summer approached, by God's grace, the river stopped being mere entertainment and started demanding that I pay attention. In fact, I vowed to sit by the river in search of reconciliation every day until God answered my call.

I embarked upon my summer's quest hoping for—and experiencing—miracles and visions. I wasn't disappointed. On day one I encountered hidden fountains in the depths of the river, portals to enchanted landscapes. Another day, thirty-five geese descended, circling before me in loving salute. These moments were the fulfillment of my long-tendered yearning to "stop and smell the roses," holding inherent value in and of themselves. But these ecstatic encounters, as it turned out, were but an all too brief respite from the challenges of everyday life.

Then one day—by many standards the least likely to inspire—something shifted. On that particular day, well into summer, I'd taken my seat by the river enjoying the serenity of the gentle flow glittering in the early morning sun. But suddenly, silent as a breath, the water began to stir as the prow of a barge came into view, pushing the water aside as it plowed through. The river held on to its smooth rolling sheets of water as long as possible as six containers, each the size of a box car, slid past my line of sight. Each was laden with hills of heavy black coal. The roaring of the motor reached my ears, the captain and crew invisible behind the equally dark windows of an elevated cabin that claimed authority over its domain. The water could no longer hold its surface and broke apart into roiling tails of white-capped surf. Long after the barge was out of sight, the river continued to churn like a storm at sea, choppy bits and pieces of muddy froth running hither and thither in all directions.

At first, I was upset—for the river and for me. After all, I came earnestly seeking serenity, not roiling waters. But then I noticed something. In truth, what the river does so well is accommodate. It accommodates the gentle breeze and the cutting bow of the ship equally. It does not judge. It lets. One moment the river is serene and placid. The next it's making way for the bulk of a six-container barge or—full of purpose—it rushes past in a tumescent current, jettisoning thirty-foot-long tree trunks in its wake. There is a grace, a simplicity, to the river's ever-changing ripples, waves, and current that shows us not only why, but how to let go and trust.

After the ship disappeared around the bend, and the churning water finally calmed back down into a gentle flow, I sat as witness to the realization that the experience of reconciliation and joy for which I yearn would not come out only as magical displays, nor out of the quest for mastery, neither in the material nor the spiritual realm. Rather, it would come out of the deep and unshakeable commitment to embrace who I am at this and every moment of my life, whatever came my way.

In the constant challenge to the status quo that aging asks of us, it is ironic that the letting go, which is often at once the most unwanted and most natural part of growing old, turns out also to be the very means of our deliverance. Even our own old dramas, our fascination with victimhood and self-importance, finally lose their power over us. We neither need approval, nor to judge. Along with the erosion of judgment, along with our very ideas of what is marginal and what is expected of us, the dichotomies finally resolve. The resolution is not an uninterrupted perfection, but an embrace of it all.

When I made my vow I thought that reconciliation of the dissonant voices would be something big—a raising up to spiritual heights. But there I sat, instead, small and insignificant. A sinking into instead of a growing larger. I did not know if I had it in me to trust that I could bring so little effort to defending the story of my life and yet have value for the world. Is it this fear that prevents us from aspiring, say, to find a comfortable chair (even one that rocks!) and read a contemplative book, to pray, to journal, or even to do something just for fun: read a rip-roaring detective novel, for heaven's sake! In our culture that privileges productivity and busyness above all, how hard is it to simply sit by the river and watch the leaves floating by—even if by doing so, we suspect that we will be led to fulfillment. Building in withdrawal from the mainstream, either as a definite break with the past, or at the very least by incorporating times of withdrawal into the fabric of your life on a regular basis, can make all the difference between being a victim of circumstances and being transformed by them. But neither does the freedom to choose to be free mean we can't respond to those organic urges that well up in us, to create, to build, to make a difference.

After months struggling to make peace between my vocation as a writer and my aspirations to be a contemplative, I am reconciled. Now as I continue my sitting practice, each discarded bottle, twig, and prow that passes by is taking something of me with it: the compulsion to be respected and adored, my worries about what things mean, my remorse over things past, and my aspirations for the future. I stopped worrying about whether I was fighting or accepting marginalization and just got on with my life—as a writer, as a contemplative, and as part of a grand family with multiple generations and dogs. Days of placid currents, days of churn. Days of serenity. Days of passion and purpose renewed. My life.

I am beginning to understand that there really is nothing to fear, for when all is stripped away, what remains is God. Today the river tells me that no matter how many days I come out to sit, pen in hand or not, and even on those days when I won't or can't come anymore, the answer will always be the same. Let. Wait. See.

Question 23

Is there a spiritually/psychologically healthy response to those times when you feel disconnected from the Sacred?

Carol Orsborn

In his inspired book *Kaddish,* Leon Weiselter writes: "There are circumstances that must shatter you; and if you are not shattered, then you have not understood your circumstances. In such circumstances, it is a failure for your heart not to break, and it is pointless to put up a fight, for a fight will blind you to the opportunity that has been presented by your misfortune."[13]

Bob and I were invited to present on the theme of spirituality and suffering at the 2014 ASA conference in San Diego. Ironically, just a few days prior to the conference, Bob slipped on black ice while walking his beloved dog, Rosie, and suffered a painful, debilitating broken shoulder. While I was assuring him long distance that I could, while reluctantly, handle the presentation on my own, Bob was busy introducing me to his old friend and collaborator, Jane Marie Thibault, the program's keynoter. It didn't take long to discover that along with sharing disappointment over Bob's unexpected absence, Jane and I had both experienced serious disruptions in our lives due to personal illness. As I wrote earlier, my life-threatening diagnosis was breast cancer eighteen years ago. Jane's more recent encounter with mortality was measured in single-digit years. Needless to say none of us had to dig too deep to bring a personal perspective to the topic of spirituality and suffering.

In her keynote presentation Jane Marie spoke honestly about her initial reaction to her diagnosis. "Do you wish to persevere pride-fully into the old life? Of course you do: the old life was a good life, but it is no longer available to you. It has been carried away, irreversibly." Jane Marie found she had to mourn: "To say Kaddish for the me who was . . . and would never be again."

Similarly, in my own experience, I have come to realize that I suffer most when I try to keep control, resist change, or force premature resolution. Acutely aware of my own losses in the difficult days following breast cancer surgery, I struggled to find any meaning or value in what I was enduring. In the journal I was keeping at the time, I wrote:

> There are those times in our lives when the pain is so great, it is enough to remind yourself to just keep breathing. I trust that in time, I will discover whether or not there is inherent meaning in what is happening to me. But I also realize

that to try to short-circuit, circumvent, or deny my pain by pretending I believe that this is some kind of gift when I clearly do not is to trivialize and degrade both myself and the Divine. Rather, I find it challenge enough simply to stay sufficiently alert to wrestle with the real questions underlying my faltering faith: Is the Divine really the source of my pain? Has God, in truth, deserted me? How am I to experience meaning in the midst of suffering?[14]

At times like these, indeed all the time as we grow older, Jane Marie suggests that we think of our lives not as a journey, but as a pilgrimage. Mature spirituality is not just about smelling the roses on an endless path. The truth is that, like it or not, we are all on our way to the same destination. Even if we dodge the reaper now, or eighteen years ago, mortality is non-negotiable. "Dignify the shock," she writes. "Sink, so as to rise."

How can we experience aging as pilgrimage? By envisioning the things that occur in later life not as a random series of sometimes positive but often negative events that have to be suffered, endured, or adapted to, but as an intentional embracing of all experiences in a movement toward wisdom, one's true self, ultimate reality, meaning, God, and one's death as final fulfillment.[15]

Paradoxically, the only way to transform the journey into a pilgrimage is to relinquish control and pray for faith. And here's the most important thing I've learned about embracing the shadow as well as the light sides of aging. We may not be able to avoid suffering—or even transform it. What we can hope to do something about is our fear.

When I'm faced with fear, I am reminded of a story I was once told about the darkest hours of the Warsaw ghetto. As Jewish families witnessed the destruction of their world, a rabbi shared words of comfort with those who turned to him with questions of meaning.

"You can weep over your suffering until you despair, or you can feel in your weeping that God weeps along with you."

This is what I experienced when I first faced my own mortality. Once I stopped struggling so hard for explanation, blame, or meaning, God found me. Eighteen years after my original diagnosis of breast cancer, this is still my God. Not God who is the source of my suffering. But rather, God who promises me that whether I am aware or not, never do I suffer alone.

Is there a spiritually/psychologically healthy response to those times when you feel disconnected from the Sacred?

Bob Weber

Am I really qualified to answer this question? Have I had times when I truly, deeply felt that God had deserted me? Have there been experiences that provoked in me, from the depths of my being, feelings such as those of the psalmist:

> *My God, My God, why have you forsaken me?*
> *Why are you so far from helping me, from the*
>   *words of my groaning?*
> *O my God, I cry by day, but you do not answer;*
> *And by night, but find no rest.*
> (PSALM 22:1–2)

If not, then I wonder why this is so, when I know so many others who have suffered feelings of abandonment by others and by God. Have I had the life of Job before all the misfortunes befell him, Job's life of prosperity and well-being? Does a similar fate await me in the future when God wagers with Satan that I will turn from him when more severe trials than I have ever experienced beset me?

I sometimes wonder whether I have just been gifted with a psychologically healthy constitution as a result of the nature and nurture I experienced in my life. This does not mean I am perfect!

The one time my faith was most profoundly shaken was the incident I discussed in an earlier section, confronting the mortality of my parents when I was seven years old. This was roughly coincident with the age the Catholic Church considers a child eligible for First Holy Communion. In other words I had reached a stage of maturity sufficient to participate more fully in the Church and understand the Eucharist sufficiently to receive it.

Despite my early confrontation with the shadow, it was the profound sense of peace and joy I knew at seven that has remained the anchor for me even at age sixty-nine, six decades later. This has only reinforced my appreciation of "Unless you become as a child, you will not enter the kingdom of heaven." Paradoxically, the spiritually/psychologically healthy response, the mature response to trying times is to once again become childlike, less encumbered by our adult minds and their productions, less burdened by our adult hearts and their cynicisms. Instead we can be filled with wonder, even while having more questions and doubts than answers and certainties. Then we can be drenched in peace and calm, not sickened by life's stormy seas. Then we can join the psalmist:

O Lord, my heart is not lifted up,
my eyes are not raised too high;
I do not occupy myself with things
too great and too marvelous for me.
But I have calmed and quieted my soul,
like a weaned child with its mother;
my soul is like the weaned child that is with me.
O Israel, hope in the Lord
From this time on and forevermore.

(PSALM 131:1–3)

Question 24

What value, if any, do those who have suffered in their aging such things as cognitive impairment and physical pain hold for us?

Bob Weber

Growing up as I did in New Jersey, I never experienced an earthquake. Hurricanes, blizzards, occasional floods, yes, but never an earthquake. Then, one day, on a vacation trip to Southern California, it happened. My wife and I were in our motel room when, all at once, the knickknacks on the shelves began to rattle and the room began to move, giving me the sense I had vertigo.

My wife, who had once lived in San Francisco, said, "An earthquake. That was an earthquake." It was a very minor tremor of an earthquake, but it created the sense that all was not well, and it certainly gave me the sense that the ground beneath our feet is not as solid as it might seem to be. In a moment my perception of the world and life changed. All of a sudden I saw life quite differently, through a different set of lenses, which provided a much clearer picture of reality.

After returning home the memory of that earthquake faded from my memory as time passed, and the impact was softened, even forgotten. Then, in the recent past, an earthquake occurred with an epicenter in Virginia, and tremors were felt in New England where I live now. Suddenly, the possibility of earthquakes was not something that occurred three thousand miles away. It was a phenomenon that was in my own backyard, close to home. Once again I look on life differently, and the perceptions and questions, the fears and the dread resurfaced, and I had to contend with them in order to get my feet back down on the ground, unsolid as it may seem to be.

Aging and its various manifestations are like the earthquakes of our lives. From the little tremors that cause the rattling of the knickknacks on the shelves, to those quakes of greater magnitude on the Richter scale, which leave an area of destruction and a house in ruins, its foundation all that is left, our world is shaken and changed forever. From the lapses of memory and other cognitive impairments, like the inability to recall a fact that was once so familiar, to the experience of not recognizing your spouse of forty years, the one sitting opposite you at the dinner table, when the onset of dementia or Alzheimer's occurs, suddenly, life does not feel as secure as it once did, the ground not as solid as it once appeared.

And after the quake what are we to do with the pain we feel as we look on the wreckage of the homes in which we have spent our lives? How can we make sense and live with the pain that wracks our bodies and our very selves? How do we bear with the arthritic pain that afflicts every joint in our bodies? What do we do with the pain of surgeries we may have had, perhaps to treat a broken hip incurred in a fall as our balance deteriorates, or to repair a knee worn and tired from years of holding us up?

Is there any value to such suffering brought on by aging? Our first reaction to this question is probably, "No!" An emphatic NO! At first sight such pain and suffering makes no sense, and we just want someone to take it away, be it the doctor, a beloved spouse or child, or God. When I wrestled with this question, the writer Louis Lavelle provided perspective on these quakes, the kind that a good seismologist would give to a trembling population. The pain and suffering cannot be eradicated, the cognitive impairments cannot necessarily be reversed, but they can take us to places we have never been before, enabling us to see as we have never seen before.

These words of Louis Lavelle from *The Dilemma of Narcissus* provide a balm for me:

> Suffering fastens upon our real being firmly and tenaciously; it cuts through all the appearances behind which we hide, until it reaches the depths of where the living self dwells. . . . We discover what we are the moment the world fails us, and what remains of ourselves when everything else is taken away. . . . It is suffering that deepens our consciousness, plowing it up, making it understanding and loving, scooping out a refuge in our souls into which the world may be welcomed. It refines to an extreme delicacy our every contact with the world. . . . And if all the suffering in the world offered us no better alternative than revolt or resignation, one might well despair of the value of the world . . . suffering acquires meaning only when it nourishes the flame of our spiritual life.[16]

What value, if any, do those who have suffered in their aging such things as cognitive impairment and physical pain hold for us?

Carol Orsborn

Lurking just beneath the surface of this question lies an underlying concern that each of us must address in our lives as we face and confront our biggest fear about aging. Are our lives only to be valued to the degree we are productive and engaged? The answer you receive to this question may and probably will change over time. At this point of my life, one of the "young old," I have the luxury of using my fear about the future as a spur to explore the depths of my faith in life and my relationship to God. I am drawn once again to the works of Thomas Merton, Abraham Joshua Heschel, Evelyn Underhill, and many others who urge us not to deny nor turn away from the pain, but to open ourselves to the possibility of making an internal shift in which the separation between one's everyday life and the Divine becomes thin, indeed.

Poet May Sarton, who suffered physically and emotionally in her last years, spoke of this embrace of both the light and the shadow in her poem "Riches Made of Loss."[17]

What are these riches? Of course, when we witness the fragility of life, we have the opportunity to that much more fervently embrace the preciousness of every moment. But there's more. Aging, at its best, puts us on a continuum of increasing loss and the potential for pain. As Dr. John C. Robinson describes: there is "a gradual fading away of identity, as if who you were or think you are is no longer very important or even that real."[18] There are memory failures, marginalization, erosion of physical and mental capabilities, and more. But Robinson suggests that these are not the obstacle but the means to fulfilling our spiritual potential. "The self-idea, or false self, created and maintained by a dense construction thought, has enshrouded the Divine Self for most of recent history. When the self-idea disappears, however, divine consciousness begins to fill and reorganize the personality in ways that transcend the ego's limited vision . . . As we wake up from the illusions of mind, we transition from personal identity to the consciousness of Divinity, giving birth to the enlightened Elder."[19]

This, I believe, is the value that contemplating those who have suffered cognitive impairment and physical pain holds for us. But what, if any, is the value of life for those who are suffering now—or to the degree that we ourselves may suffer in the future? An increasing number of people who work with individuals who have dementia every day are questioning the old paradigm—ways of judging those in their care—as tragic. Nancy Gordon of the California Lutheran Homes Center for Spirituality wrote in a much-discussed article that appeared in the American Society of Aging's *Aging Today:*

> What is it we are so afraid of? We live in a society some have labeled "hyper-cognitive"—a society that values the ability to think and remember as the highest good, and defines our worth as persons based on our cognitive abilities. . . . We don't lose our souls when our mind declines. Even when we are suffering from severe cognitive impairments we can love and be loved: we are still capable of relationship. And while we tend to equate losing cognitive function with losing everything, even when our minds aren't working we still have spirit, body and emotions—all of which are pathways for relating to others—and to God.[20]

While Nancy writes from direct observation, for many of us such a shift in perspective requires a profound leap of faith, especially when the individual diagnosed with dementia is hostile or angry, rather than passive and loving. But this is the same leap of faith that awakens in some of us an unmistakable urge toward something more than our limited judgments about everyday life in the material world. We are all on this trajectory, of course, heading toward the abyss of mortality. But make no mistake: it is a spiritual gift to be counted among those who, earlier in life, come to perceive hidden in even our greatest fears the urge toward ultimate freedom. I complete my answer to this question with a favorite quote from Evelyn Underhill's *The Mystic Way.*

> The wistful eyes of life are set towards a vision that is also a Home—a Home from which news can reach us now and again. Thus looking out from ourselves to our Universe, we seem to catch a glimpse of something behind that great pictorial cosmos of "suns and systems of suns" that more immediate world of struggle, growth, decay, which intellect has disentangled from the Abyss. We feel, interpenetrating and supporting us, the actions of a surging, creative spirit, which transcends all its material manifestations . . . Piercing its way to the surface of things, engaged, as it seems to us, in a struggle for expression, it yet transcends that which it inhabits. It is a Becoming, yet a Being, a Growth yet a Consummation: the very substance of Eternity supporting and making actual the process of Time. In such hours of lucidity we see, in fact, the faint outlines of the great paradox of Deity; as it has been perceived by the mystics of every age.[21]

In imperfection and restlessness, "the groaning and travailing of creation" we can perceive Life's urge to transcend the mundane to give expression of a higher meaning and purpose. This does not always look pretty, and neither does spiritual potential minimize the reality of the pain and suffering. But this is exactly why spiritual maturity that embraces both the shadow and the light requires an act of faith.

Question 25

How can spiritual maturity equip us to face our own unknowns?

Carol Orsborn

Pain can make a whole winter bright, like fever, force us to live deep and hard . . .

MAY SARTON

Throughout this book I have spoken about the urge to grow spiritually as the yearning to fulfill the true human potential. But as I approach this culminating question, I feel compelled to share with you one additional motivation of a somewhat darker hue. Quite simply: I do not want to die like my mother.

My mother was part of a generation of iron maidens, forged into steel by Depression and World War. This was a generation that grew into adulthood where apparent success in life was directly correlated to a potent mix of positive thinking, will, and drive. Hers was a generation in which introspection was equated to weakness or self-indulgence; religion—at best—strictly a matter of right versus wrong. This lifelong belief in self-mastery had both its strengths and weaknesses. But where the weakness became most apparent to me was in her final years.

In search of mastery in retirement, my parents moved to a gated community. Seeking comfort and security, they turned the reins of daily living over to management, who decided how loud they could play the television and forced them to remove their plants from the patio because the water hit the deck below. When my father passed away and mom began a long, painful decline, she became a victim of circumstances that increasingly spun out of her control. Words of comfort and of faith were of no help to her, for when the grit of which she was made cracked open, all that remained for her was exposure of the anxiety that had been the true bedrock of her life and profound disappointment in life and shame that she had let herself down.

As I think about my mother's experience of aging, I am humble enough to realize that I, too, will undoubtedly be faced with unknowns that will challenge me at the deepest levels. And while I, too, wish it were possible for me to have mastery of my life to the very end, I am grateful to have encountered an alternative early in life. It is, in a nutshell, Reinhold Niebuhr's seminal prayer, adopted so wisely by the twelve-step programs. "God, grant me the serenity to accept the things I cannot change, courage to change the things I can, and wisdom to know the difference."[22]

This is often easier said than done. As one of my spiritual teachers once put it, "Most people are trying to raise our comfort levels. But for seekers of wisdom, the key is rather to raise your discomfort level." As the external affirmation and ambitious busyness of my youthful life recedes, taking with it the fantasies of immortality, I am surprised and gratified that I am no longer driven by wanting to solve every dissonant note of my life. This, I recognize, is something new—something my mother could not envision nor achieve.

As I am charged to remind myself, spiritual aging does not always look like serenity. But there can be moments of transcendence: gazing at the stars and planets; celebrating the birth of a grandchild; looking into the eyes of a dog; enjoying the kindness of a cool washcloth on my forehead. As the Irish saying puts it: "Heaven is always only a half an inch above our heads."

Have I, indeed, arrived? Sometimes, transiting but half an inch is a tall order, indeed. Spiritual maturity is requiring real growth on my part, as in addition to working out the logistics of the present moment, I am also forced to prepare myself for the future even while confronting aspects of my past that I wish I'd handled better. Just as there are things I wish my mother had done differently, so it is that I am finding that the biggest spiritual challenge of all is forgiving myself.

I do believe it's some kind of progress that I am even willing to contemplate taking this all on. But do I have mastery? No. Is it a risk? Yes. Might I fail? Sadly, yes . . . but as I learned early on, if there isn't the chance of failure, it is not really a risk. Sometimes we take a leap of faith, but more frequently, we are pushed.

I have arrived at this age and stage of my life seeking a spiritual life, a simple life. But there's an irony here as well. Rather than singing with angels, I often find myself wrestling with them. But it is a divine wrestle, like Jacob on the banks of the Jabbok at Penuel Ridge. In the end, as I watch my illusions stripped away one by one, I surrender to the possibility that I may die with only one last aspiration intact: the capacity to love. Happily, this is enough.

How can spiritual maturity equip us to face our own unknowns?

Bob Weber

We shall not cease from exploration
And the end of all our exploring
Will be to arrive where we started
And know the place for the first time.

T. S. ELIOT, *FOUR QUARTETS*

Our present-day American culture does not prepare us to face the unknowns before us. We are led to avoid even looking into the void, though it lurks in the background, haunting us by its presence—especially the final unknown, death. Instead we are encouraged to look the other way, to look back to our younger years, to yearn and strive for perpetual youth, to look for ways to mask the truth of what is occurring, and to deny the truth of the clock ticking its way down to the end—that we are growing older and no amount of Botox will reverse that reality, nor will the scientific efforts to achieve immortality overcome death.

So, our culture encourages us to embrace answers that will not work and to create false hopes that will ultimately result in despair. We are not led to ask questions that will help us to grapple with the truths and realities of our human existence and that will set us on the path to fashion answers that will give us hope in the face of the unknown and the spiritual experiences to back up this hope.

When I was younger I desired to be considered a charismatic person, a person endowed and blessed with a particular gift that was unique to the world, a gift that would make me stand out in the crowd. Now that I am older, I desire to be a "prismatic" person, someone who radiates the beauty, awe, and wonder of life, whose life "refracts" an incredible rainbow that holds the potential for the lives of all people. In addition I want to be part of the group, in my case we baby boomers who are growing old and catching sight of the end of the road, to face the unknowns both alone and as one of a generation of seekers. The words of Alfred, Lord Tennyson's poem, "Ulysses," capture this vision.

> *Old age hath yet his honour and his toil;*
> *Death closes all: but something ere the end,*
> *Some work of noble note, may yet be done,*
> *Not unbecoming men that strove with Gods. . . .*
> *Tho' much is taken, much abides; and tho'*
> *We are not now that strength which in old days*
> *Moved earth and heaven, that which we are,*
> *   we are;*
> *One equal temper of heroic hearts,*
> *Made weak by time and fate, but strong in will*
> *To strive, to seek, to find, and not to yield.*

From Midlife to Afterlife

BEAR US AWAY

Throughout *The Spirituality of Age,* we have been inviting you to join us in wrestling with hard questions, in the service of deepening and cultivating a life that can be lived more fully, with anchoring faith and hope grounded in truth. We are gratified that you have chosen to join us on this journey of exploration that we have been living and sharing with one another.

Anthony de Mello's vision of spirituality has helped us frame the questions for our own inquiry—that spirituality is: (1) waking up, (2) getting rid of illusions, (3) never being at the mercy of any event, thing, or person, and (4) discovering the diamond mine inside yourself. We believe that his framework goes beyond any one religion to embrace the essence of a nearly universal progression in the spiritual—and psychological—life, the growth toward greater freedom.

By living our spiritual lives in this way, we no longer sleepwalk through life. Instead we can hope to experience and appreciate the whole of life, whatever circumstances bring our way, every moment of every day. By living this way we no longer live our lives based on lies and falsehoods. By living this way the oppressiveness of people, things, and events upon us is lightened, and we are freer to become and be who we really are, no longer contorting ourselves and becoming bent out of shape. By becoming our true selves and by being bathed in a profound sense of our belovedness—without denying or excluding any of the good, the bad, and the ugly that is within us—we can live with a sweet sense of becoming whole, including the potential to experience an expanded level of peace and joyfulness.

Having honestly explored the questions and lived our way through to the answer(s) in a way that is true for us in this moment of time, we resonate with the words of Mia Farrow who, even in the midst of her own life's challenges, found it in herself to advise: "Life is about losing everything, gracefully."[1]

Jean Vanier presents another vision of mature spirituality in his book *Community and Growth* that punctuates our questioning:

> Old age is the most precious time of life, the one nearest eternity. There are two ways of growing old. There are old people who are anxious and bitter, living in the past and illusions, who criticize everything that goes on around them. . . . But there are also old people with a child's heart, who have used their freedom from function and responsibility to find a new youth. They have the wonder of a child, but the wisdom of maturity as well. They have integrated their years of activity and so can live without being attached to power. Their freedom of heart and their acceptance of their limitations and weakness make them people whose radiance illuminates the whole community. They are gentle and merciful, symbols of compassion and forgiveness.

They become a community's hidden treasures, sources of unity and life. They are true contemplatives at the heart of community.[2]

As conversation partners and now coauthors, over the years of our growing friendship, as well as during the writing of this book, we have challenged ourselves to embrace a vision of aging and spirituality that would "go the distance."

It was more than a year into our conversations that we encountered our first big challenge. One or the other of us—and yes, we have each taken our turn a number of times over the years—was facing one of those moments when the circumstances with which we were faced temporarily outstripped our faith. As you know by now, each of us—even during the course of the writing of this book—faced everything from the loss of someone we love, to vocational and physical challenges, these and much more drawn from the shadow side of aging. What was called for was not the whitewash of a romanticized notion of suffering, and at the same time, we were beyond the zone where denial could be of any use. What we needed was a spirituality that we could not trivialize or outgrow, one that would not be outpaced by our life's circumstances. We both found it in the words and prayer of Teilhard de Chardin, which has never failed to provide comfort and consolation in the midst of the dread and a perspective that we will never outgrow, regardless of what the future holds:

Prayer for the Grace to Age Well

When the signs of age begin to mark my body
(and still more when they touch my mind);
when the ill that is to diminish me or carry me off

strikes from without or is born within me;
when the painful moment comes
in which I suddenly awaken
to the fact that I am ill or growing old;
and above all at that last moment
when I feel I am losing hold of myself
and am absolutely passive within the hands
of the great unknown forces that have formed me;
in all those dark moments, O God,
grant that I may understand that it is you
(provided only my faith is strong enough)
who are painfully parting the fibers of my being
in order to penetrate to the very marrow
of my substance and bear me away within yourself.[3]

THE LAST QUESTION: WHAT'S NEXT?

Throughout this book the focus of our twenty-five questions has been on living aging as a spiritual path. We have been most interested in mining the opportunities for spiritual growth that aging presents to us. But as Jane Marie Thibault so wisely points out, aging is also a pilgrimage. As mortals we are not just living in the present moment; we are also heading toward an unavoidable destination.

We have, in many ways, saved the most important question for the last. We humans have the capacity to do something about our deepest fears and concerns. We are able, with courage and imagination, to transform even our greatest fear to joy. We do this, as have individuals from virtually every spiritual and religious tradition through the millennia, by responding to the question: "What comes next?"

Some are fortunate in that their faith holds out a specific vision and promises of an afterlife upon which to build. For believers contemplating what comes next—their vision of heaven—can be, as Bob puts it, "Dee-licious!" For others heaven and the afterlife is, at least at this point of their lives, at most, a proactive act of imagination. But even for those of us for whom the afterlife remains a mystery, contemplating the possibilities can be, in and of itself, an act of joy. When we meet our concerns about the future, "What happens next," with faith and imagination, we give ourselves permission to be living the present moment with as much potential for joy as humanly possible.

Through the course of writing this book together, we have grown both in friendship and in faith. We do not know what the future will bring our way, but we know that because we are doing this spiritual work, we are doing everything within our power to bring about the best outcome possible. Even more to the point, together we are discovering the limits of the illusion of our life mastery, reminded by every life circumstance that comes our way, both the delightful and the uninvited, that it is ultimately God who is bearing us away. To where? May contemplation of this last question become an unfolding source of joy to you.

We sincerely hope that as you grow older, your freedom of heart and spirit, as well as the acceptance of your limitations and weakness, will allow your prismatic radiance to illuminate the whole community. We salute you as you embark on your own journey of discovery and welcome your company on our pilgrimage through this challenging and exciting new life stage.

Extraordinary Moments in Ordinary Time

W. Andrew Achenbaum, Ph.D.

I reckon late-night bull sessions to be highlights of my college years. Long past the hour in which any credible homework could be completed, two of my roommates (as if on cue) began sparring, laughing, and talking in the living room. Topics ranged from solving the world's problems, to critiquing dates and mocking professors, and to dreaming out loud about what might be in store for us after commencement.

Decades later I forget most of what was said, yet I remember the thrill of listening to fellow travelers share their impressions about the meaning of life. It was not always a comfortable experience: I had been taught at home to play the role of chameleon; I rarely found sustained introspection to be illuminating or satisfying. Nonetheless I treasured the seemingly unprecedented opportunities I had then to remove my mask. With my peers I felt diffident yet emboldened to discern truths about myself and others. I was permitted, empowered really, to voice notions of what it sincerely meant to me to be human.

Except for a few passing moments when teaching honors classes and leading graduate seminars, those exchanges during my sophomore year are the closest approximation to engaging in Plato's symposium that I ever experienced. For even at its most tipsy and outrageous, the banter was honest and revealing. Those evenings of camaraderie were love feasts: hearts and minds joined forces as late adolescents struggled to imagine and affirm how we might best prepare ourselves and help our friends to do good and to do well.

The Spirituality of Age engenders in many ways the euphoria that I once felt as I said good night to my roommates and buddies. Pages in the book never fail to yield reflections about what truly matters. Now, nearly fifty years after my sophomore year, I count myself privileged to be in the company of Bob Weber and Carol Orsborn. The pair has mastered the art and science of representing thoughts, feelings, and behavior without pretending or claiming to be sages. They know how to mentor seekers, those of us who yearn for spiritual growth and inter- (and intra-) personal substance. Carol and Bob manage to expose their vulnerabilities and admit imperfections comfortably while they impart practical wisdom. Exulting in life's joys and mysteries, Bob and Carol envision dawns that they believe still will illuminate our twilight years.

Truth be told I get more out of being a reader/listener/talker in the midst of aging boomers than I derived from nocturnal conversations in college. Few of us in the 1960s were terribly introspective; we were too busy perfecting our narcissism. None of us had seen enough or done enough to find value in doing life reviews—if we even knew what they were. We were looking forward to graduate degrees and professional programs, to solemnizing long-term relationships after graduation. For the most part we were certain that the next legs of our journeys were going to unfold in a straightforward manner—the draft notwithstanding.

As readers of *The Spirituality of Age* look in the mirror, they will doubtless see glimmers of their earlier selves. But now, there is so much more to ponder. We boomers have come a long way. We have more distance to traverse. Few of us have reached our present age without having to cope with a concatenation of losses and disappointments. Hopes have not been extinguished, however.

Boomers are fortunate if they ascertain and appreciate the abundant invitations we possess to see ourselves as we are. At the same time we can better situate ourselves in relation to others. More profoundly, many of us try to draw closer to the Ineffable. For most boomers life has not quite met our expectations (for better and for worse); our future selves are shrouded in mystery. Recognizing that roadmaps have limited utility, we seek some benchmarks and landmarks to point us on the way.

Carol Orsborn and Bob Weber offer little by way of invest-ment hints or advice for dealing with recalcitrant adult children and grandchildren. Their aim is to help us ground ourselves by focusing on the basics. The twenty-five questions posed and addressed in *The Spirituality of Age* provided me space to think about—and to compare—how similar and dissimilar my responses might be to our guides, healers by profession and vocation.

For instance, writing this afterword at the tail end of reading the book, I find myself continuing to mull my personal response to the culminating question, "How can spiritual maturity equip us to face our own unknowns?" In reading and thinking about the question, I realize that whatever spiritual maturity I have attained makes me grateful for the countless gifts and booby prizes I have been given, particularly during the third quarter of life.

Although my parents did their best to shield me and my brothers from funerals, I have been aware of death's sting for decades. I had to become increasingly mindful of the fragility of life as I buried my parents and a brother. Lately I seem to be spending more and more time reading obituaries, writing condolences, and comforting the bereaved. I myself nearly died three times—once at age seven, then at forty, more recently at fifty-five. Keenly aware of the inevitability of the finitude of my own life, I have executed legal documents to foreclose heroic interventions. I have told my daughters and remaining brother (and his son) my instructions as to how I would like my last wishes to be respected.

I have done what I can do in a prudent and thoughtful, spiritual and religious manner. I dread protracted suffering from a dehumanizing illness, but I do not fear death itself. I take to heart the truth of realizing that when I am dead, I am dead. I embrace my church's teachings about what transpires after the moment of death, although I do not comprehend much that theologians and ministers pronounce about heaven and hell. Perhaps this is why I daily read Rumi and the Psalter—they provide metaphors and images that gird me for whatever lies ahead. And I trust fellow seekers, including—most recently—Bob and Carol, to help to guide and sustain me through whatever remains of my aging journey.

From the beginning of the introductory materials with which they began this book, their nonjudgmental sensibilities and supportive sensitivities affected how I proceeded through the series of questions. The authors gave me license to amend my story as I went along. The sequence of questions suggested fresh possibilities for growth. Bob and Carol lead by example, showing us how to weave spiritual yearnings into daily activities and future goals. The fervid pursuit of spiritual connections ground them—and us—to extraordinary moments in ordinary time.

Boomers who plunge fully into *The Spirituality of Age* can allow ourselves to derive a measure of equanimity from what we read. That tranquility arises from coming to terms with where we have been amid (often failed) attempts to be intentional about where we hope to be heading. Like the coauthors, we have suffered physical pain and torturing self-doubts and medical crises and occupational disappointments. Too, we have hopes, aspirations, and unexpected joy, sometimes when we least expect it.

We can't go back to college all-night bull sessions, but we can take comfort and inspiration from spending some quality time with like-minded buddies. Like Bob and Carol, we ache to make some semblance of meaningfulness out of setbacks. We treasure affirmations with those whom we love and by whom we are cherished. And we are grateful when we encounter a book, such as *The Spirituality of Age,* that brings us—once again—to the threshold of what really matters.

W. Andrew Achenbaum, a professor of history and social work, is the Gerson and Sabina David Professor of Global Aging at the University of Houston. He also holds appointments in the Institute for Spirituality and Health, the Center for Healing and Health, is an adjunct professor in the Department of Geriatric Medicine and Palliative Care at the

University of Texas Medical Center at Houston, and in the McGovern Center for the Humanities and Ethics.

After earning degrees at Amherst College, the University of Pennsylvania, and the University of Michigan, Professor Achenbaum taught at Canisius College, Carnegie Mellon University, and the University of Michigan, where he served as deputy director of its Institute of Gerontology.

Professor Achenbaum, who has worked at the interstices of history and gerontology for more than four decades, is the author of *Old Age in the New Land, Shades of Gray, Social Security, Crossing Frontiers, Old Americans, Vital Communities,* and *Robert N. Butler, M.D.: Visionary of Healthy Aging,* and has edited/coedited six more volumes.

A past chair of the National Council on Aging, he received the Kent Award, the Gerontological Society's highest honor. At the University of Houston, Professor Achenbaum teaches a course each year on spirituality and aging.

APPENDIX

Twelve Exercises
for Seekers

As we turn to these last pages, we trust that we are leaving ourselves and our readers with both hope and mystery. As we have said earlier, one thing that is abundantly clear to us is that in having embarked upon aging as a time of spiritual growth, we are not at an end—but a beginning.

As we uncover many new questions (and happily, new answers, as well) along the way, we will continue our dialogue with one another and a growing number of individuals who share our curiosity and passion for life as it unfolds. We also have favorite spiritual exercises that we rely upon to provide us with wells of knowledge, comfort, clarity, and inspiration beyond that which our everyday problem-solving techniques had previously proven able to access.

We share some of our favorites with you here. As you will see the exercises come from a wide array of faith and spiritual traditions, reflecting both the grounding and eclectic religious, psychological, and philosophical interests of the authors. We utilize these exercises personally as well as when we lead retreats.

We trust that you will find particular exercises that call out to you and hope you will incorporate them into your own practices. We will make these exercises, and more, available at our website **www.SpiritualityofAge.com**, and hope you will share your own favorite exercises with us there.

EXERCISE 1

The Monk's Ladder

One method of spiritual exercise that has been useful to many is found in the Western Christian mystical tradition. It was first described by Guigo II, Prior of the Carthusian monastery near Grenoble in France, Le Grand Chartreuse. This monk wrote a very brief piece called, "The Ladder of the Monks." In it he described four steps for deepening the connection to God and self. In Latin the four steps are: *lectio, meditatio, oratio,* and *contemplatio.* Translated, they are "reading, meditation, prayer, and contemplation."

Put simply, the first step of the Monk's Ladder is to select a passage from sacred literature, such as the scriptures, and read it slowly, as if you were biting into an entrée prepared by a fine chef. Then meditate on the passage as if you were slowly chewing the bite you had taken while beginning to appreciate the variety of tastes and their complexity. Next pray in reaction to the tastes and their complexity—perhaps a sigh of "Ahhhh!" Finally contemplate the experience by simply "savoring" the dish you are experiencing, without words.

You can apply the Monk's Ladder technique to yourself by approaching your own life's questions as sacred text. For example, you may find yourself asking any of the following:

How am I to read the signs of the times as I age, and what am I to do in the face of them?

What is to become of me now that my physical health is changing?

What am I to do and what will I be now that my career is ending and familiar roles will no longer be available to me?

What am I to do with the suffering I experience at the loss of family, friends, and peers?

As you move through the questions arising in your life, the Monk's Ladder technique encourages you to not just react to what you experience. You will be led to respond with deeper appreciation of the spiritual opportunities that are in store for you. Here's what you can expect when you apply the Monk's Ladder to your questions as they arise:

- You will listen more closely to what is really happening. You will slowly begin to hear that to which you are listening, in more attuned ways, without missing the subtleties and details.

- You will be invited to respond to your experience in a deeper way, reacting neither to your anxieties and fears, nor to your wishes and yearning for quick and easy answers.

- Finally you will become more peaceful and content to rest in the moment, savoring the spiritual flavor of your experience.

Those more attuned and practiced in Eastern approaches to spiritual exercise will notice similarities to "mindfulness" practice. Both result in a deeper appreciation of what is happening in the moment, as you try to make sense of it and find the meaning for which you hunger in the midst of life's perplexing and challenging questions.

EXERCISE 2

Take Your Question for a Walk

In daily life we are used to approaching questions by relying upon the left side of our brain: utilizing logic, will, and rational thought. When it comes to questions of spirit, however, we need to rely on another mode of being: tapping our right brain intuition and making ourselves receptive to the Divine. The challenge for many of us is that unlike with rational thinking, we can't make wisdom and inspiration perform on cue. In fact, the best we can do is make ourselves ready to receive.

One way to do this is to take your question for a walk in nature. This is not simply a hike or a stroll. Approach this as a spiritual exercise, and you will find yourself accessing sources of wisdom that affirm, reveal, and deepen your relationship to the sacred.

Set aside at least an hour when you can be alone and unpressured. Pick a place for your walk that is pleasant and familiar, such as a favorite park or a path around a lake.

Before you go write down the question for which you'd most like to receive an answer on a piece of paper. Take the question deeply into your heart as you write it down, thinking about why this particular question is important to you and how grateful you will be for insight, guidance, and the answer.

Crumple up the paper and throw it away. As you do put the question entirely out of your conscious mind. Instead, as you walk, put your attention on the wonders of nature. Let your eyes be drawn to whatever catches your curiosity or appreciation: a flower growing out of a rock, a worm slowly making its way across a stick. Enjoy the abundance around you without needing anything out of it, neither judging nor demanding, while entertaining a mood of receptivity.

Above all don't think about the question you had in mind at the beginning of the walk. If it tries to push its way to the fore, acknowledge it, thank it, and release it.

Doing this opens up the optimum space for your intuition to surface the answer you seek. When it pops into your mind, it will have a different quality than answers that have been forced or figured out. This is the "Eureka" experience Archimedes experienced in his bathtub when discovering water displacement as the fundamental of physics. It may be triggered by something you have encountered on your walk, or it may came to you "out of the blue," an experience Carol refers to in her retreats as "thunderstruck."

By walk's end you will have the answer to your question. You will either have been graced with new insights, direction, and certainty. Or the answer to your question will be that the time is not yet ripe for you to know and that wisdom is asking you to trust in the unfolding of time.

Spirit works invisibly. It is like a river, flowing freely until it hits an obstacle. Then it pauses—pooling up upon itself—until it rises high enough to push over to the other side. The I Ching, the ancient Chinese book of wisdom, teaches what you have observed for yourself: If increase goes on cumulatively, there is bound to be a breakthrough.[1] The time you spent on this walk is like water filling up behind the dam. Remember, if you try to look for the dammed water from the other side of the wall, you cannot see it rise until one last drop carries it over the top. Similarly, inner work, done with good intentions, is never wasted. Every drop contributes to growing your wisdom, whether or not you are in a position yet to reap the rewards. It is a totally efficient process. The surest way to the answer you seek is to be fully where you are right now, regardless of the results you have or haven't gotten. If you received the answer you'd hoped for, at walk's end, stop and give thanks. If you haven't, give thanks anyway, and then simply do what's next.

EXERCISE 3

The Vision Test

As you know by now we have put being at peace farther down on the list of aspirations as we age than other qualities and characteristics, such as embracing both the shadow and the light and waking up to being more fully alive. In this exercise we are going to ask you to build a vision of what a psychologically and spiritually healthy old age could look like for you. This exercise has two parts.

PART ONE

Read through the following list of questions. Then close your eyes and imagine your life in extreme old age in as much detail as possible.

How do you feel emotionally?

What are you thinking?

What are you sensing?

Are you giving and receiving love?

Are you aware of the presence of the Divine?

What's most important to you?

Anything else you'd like to build into your vision of a psychologically and spiritually healthy old age?

When you've completed part one of this exercise, open your eyes, and write down what you imagined in as much detail as possible. When you've captured your portrait of old age, you are ready for part two.

PART TWO

Go through the list again and underline any quality or characteristic that is NOT dependent on external circumstances: for instance, a sense of humor versus the ability to run a marathon. And here's the payoff. The more items you have underlined, the more likely you are to have a healthy attitude about aging now. You have a solid spiritual, emotional, and psychological foundation upon which to build. If you have fewer items underlined than you'd like, add to this list over time. Actively observe elders who, regardless of the external challenges with which they are faced, have the kind of relationship with aging you'd like to have for yourself.

This is your master list. Keep this list with you as you face both the challenges and opportunities that come your way, remembering that the items on this list are nonnegotiable, comprising the core of aspirations that will lead you to inner freedom.

EXERCISE 4

How Are You Called?

In Isaiah 43 it is written: "I have called you by name, you are mine." Think about your name and what it has to teach you about your relationship with the Divine. In the Jewish tradition one is given a Hebrew name at birth. As mentioned earlier, the translation of Carol's Hebrew name means "life and joy." However, many of us, including Carol, have had many names over the years, representing a number of external and internal influences. For instance, she has at times used or left off her middle name, adopted her husband's name, added titles. In all, she's had eight significant name changes over her lifespan, each reflecting her values and evolution of spiritual understanding at that stage in life.

When many individuals do this exercise, they often encounter emotional linkages (pride or rejection) to saint namesakes, biblical and sacred text references, and more. Other names reflect a legacy in the practice of a particular trade, bespeaking the intimacy between generations, or a relationship to something out of the natural world.

So, what does your name have to tell you? You can explore this by pondering the following questions:

Who gave you your name?

Does your original name tell you something about the influences/expectations placed upon you by others?

Were there role models you were meant to emulate?

What inspired the changes (or lack of changes) you made along the way?

Did you take on (or were you given) a nickname?

What does the name you use today tell you about where you've come from, your growing relationship with the Divine, and your take on how you ought to live?

If the Divine were to call you by name now, what would that name be?[2]

EXERCISE 5

Look in the Mirror

This exercise has three parts.

PART ONE

Next time you step out of the shower, take a long, loving look in the mirror. Who do you see when you look in the mirror? Don't just take in your graying hair and wrinkles. See not only yourself in the present moment, but everybody and everything that has contributed to making you who you are today.

Lovingly recall the people who enabled you to become who you are as you look at what you see reflected back that you appreciate about yourself. Pay particular attention to the details of your recollections, especially the specific thoughts and feelings that emerge from your memory. Do you see the twinkle in your eyes? The upturn of your mouth in a smile? What sense do they create within you?

Remember those men and women whom you idealized. What aspects of them did you incorporate into your own emerging sense of yourself? What aspects enabled you to become more yourself? When and how did you get closer to the best in them and your true self?

PART TWO

Imagine a scene with a loved one in your life where you knew you were loved by what he or she said, felt, or did. Now imagine you are embraced by the Divine with unmistakable love. Write down the details of your experience of this moment. What is your response to this experience? How does this make you feel? What does it lead you to think and to understand?

PART THREE

Return to the mirror and see if you now experience yourself any differently.

EXERCISE 6

Image of the Divine

This is a two-part exercise.

PART ONE

Recall your earliest images of the Divine, and focus on the one image that predominated for you. What was the fruit of this image—fear, dread, shame, guilt—or peace, relief, comfort, freedom?

How did this representation of the Divine come into being for you? What people, institutions, and experiences contributed to this image?

PART TWO

At this time of your life, now what is your image of the Divine? Does this image help you to live more fully and to deal more peacefully with the circumstances of your life, regardless of what they are?

Can you identify what experiences and people gave rise to this new image?

EXERCISE 7

Intimacy with the Sacred: A Timeline

This exercise has four parts.

Sometimes spirituality exists independently of religion; sometimes religion exists apart from spirituality. But there are those moments when the two converge. How have these strands of relationship to the Divine been intertwining in your life, and what can you learn from their relationship over time?

PART ONE

To do this exercise get a piece of white paper and four colored pencils. Along the bottom of the sheet, draw a timeline of your life with one of the colors, marked off in ten-year segments.

PART TWO

Now pick another color and draw a line parallel to the first one, to indicate those years in which you have been "religious." This may be a solid line all the way across, or it may be broken into pieces, such as indicating that you were religious from ages zero to ten, then nothing again until you were fifty. You may also have no line at all.

PART THREE

Now pick a third color, this time representing your spirituality, and draw a third line parallel to the first and second. Again, this may be a solid line all the way across, or it may be broken into pieces, such as indicating that you were spiritual from ages twenty to thirty, then nothing again until you were sixty. You may also have no line at all.

PART FOUR

Finally pick a fourth color, this time representing your intimacy with the Divine, and draw a fourth line parallel to the first, second, and third. Again, this may be a solid line all the way across, or it may be broken into pieces, such as indicating that you were most intimate with the Divine from ages ten to twenty, then nothing again until you were forty. You may also have no line at all.

Once you are done take a look at the chart you've drawn. When have you been most intimate with the Divine? Does it coincide more with those times you have been religious but not spiritual, spiritual but not religious, neither or both?

EXERCISE 8

Snapshot of Your Life

This is a two-part exercise.

PART ONE

Take some time to go through scrapbooks of photos of yourself at earlier stages of your life, perhaps one for each decade. Let yourself be drawn to a half dozen or more that really speak to you: evoking feelings in you of what it was like to be at that age, circumstance, and stage in your life.

Now ask yourself, as pictured in each photo, the following questions:

What were you alive to?

What were you asleep to?

What more was there yet to awaken to that you were unaware of at the time?

PART TWO

Now find a recent photo, one that speaks to you, and ask yourself these three questions:

What are you alive to?

What are you asleep to?

What more is there yet to awaken to of which you are unaware?

EXERCISE 9

Awakenings: An Inventory

This exercise has multiple steps to it.

PART ONE

First make a list of one or more major awakenings in your life.

If you have only one awakening, take a moment to describe your life before the awakening and your life following. Would you say that you have had a definitive awakening? If so, what have you awakened to? If you can answer this question to your satisfaction, you are done with this exercise.

PART TWO

If you can't answer the question above to your satisfaction, or if you have already listed more than one awakening, read on.

Draw a spiral with at least seven turns on it. (These turns do not equate to specific spans of time, such as a year or decade, but rather provide a generalized metaphor for the sweep of your life.)

Without overthinking it place an "X" on the spot where you sense yourself to be on your life spiral right now. Are you on an upswing, heading toward a new peak? Or are you in or just leaving a trough? Wherever you think you are right now, mark it down.

Finally go back to your list and place the awakenings that you have numbered on your list on the chart. Do your awakenings tend to occur at the troughs or at the peaks—both or perhaps even in between?

Is there a pattern to where they have occurred in the past? Do you have the sense that there will be more awakenings in your future?

EXERCISE 10

Making Amends

In *The Gift of Years,* author Joan Chittister writes,

> One of the functions—one of the gifts—of aging is to become comfortable with the self we are, rather than to mourn what we are not. It is a moment of enlightenment when we realize that the years have grown us as well as sustained us. We are of more substance now than we were when we were young, whatever we did in the past, wherever we were when we did it. The fact is that twinges of regret are a step-over point in life. They invite us to revisit the ideals and motives that brought us to where we are now.[3]

It is at this point, at last, that you have made amends for everything of the past that is rectifiable and have become firmly committed to addressing new causes for remorse in the present moment as you encounter them and as they occur. As the twelve-step programs teach us, you come to accept that there are things you cannot change; you have the courage to change the things you can; and you have growing wisdom that enhances your ability to recognize the difference. At this point you stop living your life by looking only in the rearview mirror and point your nose back into the heat of life. In the present moment, as we wrote earlier, you can find it is serious and constructive enough to sometimes or even often ponder the mystery of the stars and planets, the birth of a child, the love radiating from the eyes of a favorite pet. You become, in fact, not only a person who takes his or her spiritual and psychological growth seriously, but you become a mystic.

This is a four-step exercise. Do one step at a time and resist the urge to read ahead.

1. Write down ten of your biggest regrets, occasions for guilt or shame that you still carry with you. After you've written them down, return for step 2.

2. Circle every item on the list that you are able to do something about: offer an apology, make amends, or rectify in some way or other. When you are done with this list, make a commitment to yourself to do so as courageously, sensitively, and quickly as possible.

3. Underline everything else on the list.

4. Release each of the underlined items in whatever way you deem appropriate. You may want to write them down on a separate list and burn them. You may want to bless and release every item by imagining each one growing

wings and flying off into the distance. Bring creativity and compassion to yourself, with equal amounts of forgiveness and acceptance, as you release all that no longer serves you.

EXERCISE 11

To What Are You Called?

Think of someone you've met personally, or in literature or history, who illustrates the notion of tikkun, the Jewish belief that it is the individual's task to retrieve shattered shards of goodness and light and bring their contribution back to help repair the world. What adjectives, qualities, and characteristics best describe the essence of the individual you chose as someone who represents tikkun to you? Take a moment to make a list of these descriptors before reading on.

ANALYSIS

The list you came up with says as much about you as it does about the person you selected. The particular words you chose to describe someone who represents tikkun give you a vivid, concrete profile of the aspirations you hold in regard to what you aspire to awaken to. Not every word you put on the list may apply to you, but the list—as a whole—will provide you with interesting insights about yourself and what gives your life meaning and purpose, regardless of the circumstances you may face over the coming years. In fact, when it comes to retrieving shards of light—doing the sacred work of tikkun—it could well be argued that the greater the shadows with which you are confronted as you age, the greater the contribution toward repair of the world you have the potential to make.

EXERCISE 12

The Next Chapter

Think about your spiritual progression through life as chapters in your spiritual autobiography. You don't need to write out each chapter. For the purposes of this exercise, giving each chapter an apt title is enough.

Chapter One describes the spiritual worldview into which you were born. If you were to give this chapter a title, what would it be? Now think about what happened next: Did you go through a state of rebellion? Was there a time when you more fully embraced the beliefs into which you were born? Perhaps you found an alternate community that allowed you to deepen your experience of your faith?

Your book may be three chapters, ten chapters, or as many as you need to fully tell your story. However many chapters you choose, give each one a title and write it down.

Now, if you haven't done so already, add a last chapter to the book: your spiritual aspirations, hopes, and beliefs about the future. Feel free to define "future" as you wish, to take you through to the end of life and beyond. You can simply give this a title or take the time to write out the chapter in full.

Recommended Reading

Full publication details for all of the books listed here are given in the bibliography. The following summaries include publisher's descriptions as well as coauthors' commentary.

Aging as a Spiritual Practice: A Contemplative Guide to Growing Older and Wiser, by Lewis Richmond. Teacher Lewis Richmond brings the Buddhist perspective to aging in this helpful book. Richmond writes: "Elderhood is the culminating stage of a life fully lived. When the time comes, we can (although we may not always) assume the mantle of elderhood as a kind of birthright. . . . These days, each of us has to imagine and construct our own expression of elderhood, and find ways to bring it forward." Aging carries with it loss, and the loosening of identification with individual ego. Buddhism, with its emphasis on dis-illusionment, views aging as holding the potential to serve as a spiritual path.

Aging: The Fulfillment of Life, by Henri J. M. Nouwen and Walter J. Gaffney. In *Aging*, Henri Nouwen and Walter Gaffney share some moving and inspirational thoughts on what aging means (and can mean) to all of us, whether we're in our youth, middle age, or in our later years. This book shows how to make the latter years a source of hope rather than a time of loneliness—a way out of darkness, into the light. They remind us of our responsibility to incorporate the aged into the fabric of our own lives—helping them become teachers again so they may help us repair the fragmented connections between generations.

At Eighty Two: A Journal by May Sarton, by May Sarton. Written just a few years before her death, this book balances the realities of the poet/writer Sarton's increasingly challenging days with the optimistic musings of a contemplative. Chronicling both the mundane and the sublime, May is self-revealing as well as generous as she records the frustrations of physical frailty while engaged with a mind still agile and curious. This book, and all of Sarton's previous journals for that matter, remind us that we need not live nor record romanticized notions of our journeys for our lives to be meaningful.

Contemplative Aging: A Way of Being in Later Life, by Edmund Sherman. *Contemplative Aging* is for men and women age sixty and beyond who want to experience a more peaceful, aware way of being through contemplative practices and to transcend the many causes of suffering inherent in later life.

The December Project: An Extraordinary Rabbi and a Skeptical Seeker Confront Life's Greatest Mystery, by Sara Davidson. At eighty-five, Rabbi Zalman Schachter-Shalomi asked writer Sara Davidson to have an ongoing conversation about how people can navigate the December of life and to help them "not freak out about dying." This book includes deep insight, honest vulnerability, and spiritual exercises to aid readers in experiencing a sea change in facing their mortality.

A Deepening Love Affair: The Gift of God in Later Life, by Jane Marie Thibault. Jane Thibault's book is for all of those who yearn for something more in their life. That something more, the author contends, is the gift of an intimate relationship with God. This gift may be received at any time in life, but according to the author's observations and studies, the older person is best suited to fully enter into this relationship. This book deals with the inner work that is the spiritual life task of the mature adult. The author is convinced that God has saved the best for last!

Falling Upward: A Spirituality for the Two Halves of Life, by Richard Rohr. Richard Rohr shares his own aging process with us in ways that help us be less afraid of ours. He helps to see that, as we grow older, we can wake up to the profound mysteries of life, realities we could not see or appreciate in our youth.

Finding Meaning in the Second Half of Life: How to Finally, Really Grow Up, by James Hollis. James Hollis takes on the question: What does it really mean to be a grown-up in today's world? He believes that it is only in the second half of life that we can truly come to know who we are and thus create a life that has meaning. He provides a crucial bridge across this critical passage of adult development.

The Five Stages of the Soul, by Harry R. Moody and David Carroll. The coauthors take us on an exciting exploration of the spiritual passages we go through as we age—from midlife crisis to the search for inner purpose—and the rich possibilities they offer for fulfillment in the life journey. Interweaving psychology, religion, myth, and literature, Moody charts the passages of countless individuals across the country, who have journeyed through the five stages of spiritual awakening common to almost all of us: the Call, the Search, the Struggle, the Breakthrough, and finally, the Return. He offers readers a detailed roadmap of their quest for meaning and self-discovery.

From Age-ing to Sage-ing: A Profound New Vision of Growing Older, by Zalman Schachter-Shalomi. This book by the late respected rabbi Zalman Schachter-Shalomi marries spirituality, intellectual grounding, and practical application. Faced with his own fears about aging, the rabbi went on a vision quest where he encountered the help and wisdom of Sufi masters, Buddhist teachers, brain-mind research, and Native American shamans. The book is full of zest, inspiration, and life. But not without a price. The book also addresses the importance of coming to terms with death and dying, reminding us that at the base of our fears about aging are our unprocessed feelings about mortality.

A Generation of Seekers: The Spiritual Journeys of the Baby Boom Generation, by Wade Clark Roof. *A Generation of Seekers* takes a revealing look at the "boomer culture" and their search for meaning and values in a complex world. We boomers were spiritually shaken by the 1960s, felt aftershocks of the 1970s, and by our very numbers alone, remain a battering ram for social change. Roof gives the backstory and sociological perspective to this.

The Gift of Years: Growing Older Gracefully, by Joan Chittister. Sister Joan Chittister is clear-eyed about both the challenges and possibilities inherent in aging. Her chapter on "Regret" is required reading for all of us who have unfinished business with the past. She writes: "The thought of what could have been eats at the center of the heart. It pretends to be reflection, a kind of tally of the years. But down deep it feels more like failure than it does understanding. . . . Regret is a temptation. It entices us to lust for what never was in the past rather than to bring new energy to our changing present."

Hymns to an Unknown God: Awakening the Spirit in Everyday Life, by Sam Keen. Written while Sam was in his sixties, this classic challenges readers to question every aspect of our lives and identities constructed over the course of our lives, and open ourselves to the mysteries and possibilities of a larger reality. Writes Keen: "Much of the turmoil of my life has come from struggling to actualize some fantasy or realize an ideal of self that is unfitting . . . but then in an instant, my perspectives shift, and I accept what before was problematic. I view my history, my parents, my body type, my strange appetite for asking questions, and my unsettled and unsettling mind as my destiny. What was a wound is transformed into a gift."

Life Gets Better: The Unexpected Pleasures of Growing Older, by Wendy Lustbader. Wendy Lustbader's rich collection of stories about the men and women with whom she has worked distills their wisdom, offering us valuable insights through their lived experience. A consummate professional, this role does not bridle her humanity. Wendy's empathy and compassion for her clients open our eyes to the uniqueness of our common human suffering and to the possibilities for transcendence.

The Measure of My Days: One Woman's Vivid, Enduring Celebration of Life and Aging, by Florida Scott-Maxwell. Florida, also in her eighties, takes a deep, unvarnished dive into the meaning of her life in old age and reemerges triumphant. A Jungian analyst, Florida writes: "Age puzzles me. I thought it was a quiet time. My seventies were interesting, and fairly serene, but my eighties are passionate. I grow more intense as I age." There is a shadow side to this, as Florida writes "we also find that as we age we are more alive than seems convenient, or even bearable." Ultimately, Florida shows us the way to become "fierce with reality."

Pilgrimage into the Last Third of Life: 7 Gateways to Spiritual Growth, by Jane Marie Thibault and Richard L. Morgan. The last third of life (age sixty and beyond) offers significant challenges that Thibault and Morgan propose we approach as a pilgrimage. Their scripture-based meditations and reflection questions examine seven tasks essential to living the last third fearlessly and with purpose: facing aging and dying, learning to live with limitations, doing inner work, living in and out of community, prayer and contemplation, redeeming loss and suffering, and leaving a legacy.

Remembering Your Story: Creating Your Own Spiritual Autobiography, by Richard L. Morgan. This book offers readers of all ages a way to create their own spiritual autobiographies. Helpful to small groups as well as individuals, this resource leads you through ten weeks of study that include such topics as: life stories, reclaiming childhood stories, family relationships, stories that connect the generations, and healing of memories.

The Return of the Prodigal Son: A Story of Homecoming, by Henri Nouwen. Nouwen, Catholic priest and scholar, descends into the trenches of family relationships. He views his own life through multiple symbolic lenses, including identifying with both elder and younger siblings, father and son. The book is based on both the

Christian parable of The Prodigal Son and the painting by Rembrandt, which, in the words of *New Oxford Review* speaks to us "in the terrible beauty of the transformation to which it calls us."

Second Journeys: The Dance of Spirit in Later Life, edited by Bolton Anthony. The thirty-eight essays in this anthology, including one by Carol Orsborn, cover a wide range of subjects by top authors in the Conscious Aging movement. These include: "Second Journeys," "Aging as a Spiritual Practice," "Serving from Spirit," and "Rites of Passage into Elderhood." Bolton Anthony of SecondJourney.org served as editor along with contributing editors Ron Pevny, Ellen B. Ryan, Claudia Moore, and Randy Morris.

Spiritual Marketplace: Baby Boomers and the Remaking of American Religion, by Wade Clark Roof. Wade Clark Roof returned to interview people at midlife from his study that led to *A Generation of Seekers.* He noted a shift away from religion as traditionally understood to more diverse and creative approaches. He found a unique set of spiritual values and charted the emergence of five subcultures among these older boomers: dogmatists, born-again Christians, mainstream believers, metaphysical believers and seekers, and secularists.

Spirituality and Aging, by Robert C. Atchley. This book incorporates material from two decades of interviews, observations, study, and reflection to illustrate ways of thinking about and discussing spirituality—what it is, why it is important, and how it influences the experience of aging. It provides a nuanced view of spirituality and the richness it brings to the lives of older people.

Staring at the Sun: Overcoming the Dread of Death, by Irvin D. Yalom. Not technically a book about aging, this powerful book by psychotherapist Irvin Yalom reveals how knowledge of our own mortality affects the unconscious mind of every human being at every stage of life, especially acute in old age. Yalom, who wrote this book in his seventies, teaches that denial of death is the root cause of our fears, stresses, and depression. He adapts words from

Nietzsche to summarize the way to transcendence: "To become wise you must learn to listen to the wild dogs barking in your cellar."

The Three Secrets of Aging: A Radical Guide, by John C. Robinson. This powerful little book by interfaith minister John Robinson goes even further than describing aging as a spiritual path. Robinson contends that aging, itself, can be a mystical experience. He views the longevity revolution as comprising an entirely new stage of evolution: a transformation of self and consciousness, and a revelation of a new and sacred world. "We age not to get sick and die in misery but to progressively transform self and consciousness to rediscover Heaven on Earth," writes Robinson.

Who Am I . . . Now That I'm Not Who I Was? Conversations with Women in Mid-Life and the Years Beyond, by Connie Goldman. Connie, in her eighties, interviewed eighteen women between the ages of fifty-two and eighty-seven, who provide us with extraordinary role models of self-acceptance and gracious aging. But it is Connie's voice itself that carries the book's central message: that aging is an opportunity to not only grow older, but to grow whole. From the introduction: "The journey in between who you once were and who you are now becoming is where the dance of life really takes place."

Winter Grace: Spirituality and Aging, by Kathleen Fischer. Fischer writes in her introduction, "The later years take us into the heart of the central Christian paradox of death/resurrection. It is in living the pattern of that mystery that people discover the graces of life's winter season and share them with all of us."

Notes

FOREWORD. SUMMONS TO A LEAP OF FAITH

1. Rilke, *Letters to a Young Poet,* 35.

CHAPTER 1. AGING AS THE PATH
TO SPIRITUAL MATURITY

1. Cumming and Henry, *Growing Old.*

2. Ibid.

3. Havighurst and Albrecht, *Older People;* Lemon, Bengtson, and Peterson, "An Exploration of the Activity Theory of Aging," 511–23.

4. Maddox, "Disengagement Theory," 80–83.

5. Becker, *The Denial of Death.*

6. Nouwen and Gaffney, *Aging.*

7. Jacoby, *Never Say Die,* 190–92.

8. Erikson, *The Life Cycle Completed,* 61–66.

9. Eliot, "The Four Quartets," 117.

10. Rilke, *Letters to a Young Poet,* 18–19.

11. Ibid., 34–35.

12. Larson, *The Far Side Gallery 2,* 14.

13. Rumi, "The Guest House," 109.

14. Lynch, *Christ and Apollo,* 27–33.

CHAPTER 2. OUR SPIRITUAL BIOGRAPHIES

1. Puhl, *The Spiritual Exercises of St. Ignatius.*
2. Goldman, in private conversation at the American Society of Aging 2011 annual conference, paraphrased from her book *Who Am I . . . Now That I'm Not Who I Was?*

CHAPTER 3. THE SEEKER'S GUIDE

1. Rabbi Nathan Siegel, Rosh Shoshana sermon at Marin County Jewish Community Center, 1991.
2. Puhl, *The Spiritual Exercises of St. Ignatius,* 141–50.
3. Maimonides, *Guide to the Perplexed.*
4. Hollis, *Finding Meaning in the Second Half of Life.*

CHAPTER 4. WHAT IS SPIRITUAL MATURITY?

1. Orsborn, private journal, 2012, paraphrased in Orsborn, *Fierce with Age,* 201–2.
2. Finley, paraphrase of evening meditation and talk on Meister Eckhardt at St. Monica's Catholic Community, Los Angeles, July 19, 2012.
3. Mello, *Walking on Water,* 83.
4. Young-Eisendrath and Miller, *The Psychology of Mature Spirituality.*
5. Erikson, *The Life Cycle Completed,* 61–66.
6. Kula and Loewenthal, *Yearnings.*
7. Merton, *No Man Is an Island,* 133.
8. Feinstein and Krippner, *The Mythic Path* and *Personal Mythology.*
9. Bridges, *Transitions,* 119.
10. Rizzuto, *The Birth of the Living God.*
11. Puhl, *The Spiritual Exercises of St. Ignatius,* 154–56.
12. Cox, interviewed by Allis in "Finding Their Religion."
13. Steinfels, "Charting the Currents of Belief for the Generation that Rebelled."
14. Roof, *Spiritual Marketplace,* back cover copy.

15. Ibid.
16. Carlin, quoted in Wit & Wisdom, *The Week,* February 10, 2012, 17.
17. Mello, *Walking on Water,* 83.
18. MacMurray, quoted by Barry, SJ, in "The Kingdom of God and Discernment," 157.
19. Smull and Orsborn, *The Silver Pearl.*
20. Haronian, "The Repression of the Sublime," 51–62.
21. Ibid.
22. Ibid.

CHAPTER 5. WHAT IS SPIRITUAL AWAKENING?

1. Personal communication.
2. Thomas, "Do not go gentle into that good night."
3. Faulkner, "The Bear," *The Saturday Evening Post,* May 9, 1942.
4. Unamuno, BrainyQuote.com, http://www.brainyquote.com/quotes/m/migueldeun106560,html (accessed, April 27, 2015).
5. Rinpoche, quoted by Yalom in *Staring at the Sun,* 155.
6. Lessing, quoted by Orsborn in *The Art of Resilience,* 6.
7. Merton, *The Silent Life,* Farrar, Strauss and Giroux ed., 127–44.
8. Gunn, *Journey to Emptiness.*
9. Farrer-Halls, *The Illustrated Encyclopedia of Buddhist Wisdom,* 7.
10. McCartney, "Let It Be."
11. Wilhelm and Baynes, *The I Ching.*
12. Friedman, private conversation, 2011, and "Shever v'Tikkun/Shattering and Repair."
13. Ibid.
14. Ibid.
15. Merton, *The Silent Life,* Farrar, Strauss and Giroux ed., 127–44.
16. Kohut and Wolf, "The Disorders of the Self and Their Treatment," 55.
17. Ibid.
18. Nouwen, "Being the Beloved," a sermon delivered at Robert Schuller's Crystal Cathedral, Garden Grove, California, November 22, 2012.

19. Chittister, *The Gift of Years,* 5.

20. Midler, "What I Know Now."

21. Chittister, *The Gift of Years,* 3.

22. Ibid.

CHAPTER 6. WHAT IS FREEDOM?

1. Dullea, "Enough is Enough for Ex-Superwoman."

2. Malraux, *The Walnut Trees of Altenburg,* 74.

3. Hollis, *Finding Meaning in the Second Half of Life,* 29.

4. Ibid., 40.

5. Ibid.

6. Short, *The Gospel According to Peanuts,* 86.

7. Unamuno, BrainyQuote.com, www.brainyquote.com/quotes/m/
   migueldeun106560,html (accessed, April 27, 2015).

8. Spielberg, *War Horse.*

9. Claudel, quoted by Cowley in *The View from 80,* 17.

10. Robinson, *The Three Secrets of Aging,* 65–66.

11. Orsborn, *The Art of Resilience,* 209.

12. Feinstein and Krippner, *Personal Mythology,* quoted by Smull and
    Orsborn in *The Silver Pearl,* 219.

CHAPTER 7. HOW CAN WE BECOME
MORE FULLY OURSELVES?

1. Camus, quoted in Wit & Wisdom, *The Week,* November 1, 2013, 15.

2. Santayana, quoted in Wit & Wisdom, *The Week,* November 1,
   2013, 15.

3. Roosevelt, quoted in Wit & Wisdom, *The Week,* November 1,
   2013, 15.

4. Weber, "Unraveling Projective Identification and Enactment,"
   71–83.

5. Goldman, in private conversation at the American Society of Aging
   2011 annual conference, paraphrased from her book: *Who Am I . . .
   Now That I'm Not Who I Was?*

6. Keen, *Hymns to an Unknown God,* quoted in Orsborn, *Fierce with Age,* 201–2.

7. Levinson, *The Seasons of a Man's Life,* 59–60.

8. Finley, paraphrase of evening meditation and talk on Meister Eckhardt at St. Monica's Catholic Community, Los Angeles, July 19, 2012.

9. Ibid.

CHAPTER 8. WHAT IS THE VALUE OF AGING TO SOCIETY?

1. Moody, "Conscious Aging."

2. Erikson, *Wisdom and the Senses,* 187.

3. Erikson, *The Life Cycle Completed,* 61–66.

4. Moody, "Conscious Aging."

5. Merton, *The Seven Story Mountain,* 347.

6. Ibid, 362.

7. Senior, *The Joys of Getting Older,* back cover quotes.

8. Leiber and Stoller, "Is That All There Is?" Recording released by Peggy Lee, 1969.

9. Lustbader, *Life Gets Better.*

10. Thibault, "Aging as a Natural Monastery," 5.

11. Merton, *No Man is an Island,* 133.

12. Finley, *Merton's Palace of Nowhere,* 51.

13. Weiselter, *Kaddish,* 226.

14. Orsborn, personal journal, 1997.

15. Thibault, "Aging as a Natural Monastery," paraphrased in her keynote address at the American Society of Aging annual conference, March 13, 2014.

16. Lavelle, *The Dilemma of Narcissus,* 102–5.

17. Sarton, "Riches Made of Loss," in *Collected Poems: 1930–1973,* 409–10.

18. Robinson, *The Three Secrets of Aging,* 60.

19. Ibid.

20. Gordon, "In-the-Moment Connecting with Dementia Patients Reaps Rewards," 11.

21. Underhill, *The Mystic Way,* 4–5.

22. Niebuhr, quoted in *Grapevine,* 6–7.

CONCLUSION. FROM MIDLIFE TO AFTERLIFE

1. Farrow, quoted in Wit & Wisdom, *The Week,* October 18, 2013, 17.

2. Vanier, *Community and Growth,* 140–41.

3. Teilhard de Chardin, "Prayer for the Grace to Age Well," 178.

APPENDIX. TWELVE EXERCISES FOR SEEKERS

1. Rogala and Orsborn, *Trust, Inc.*

2. Baynes and Wilhelm, *The I Ching.*

3. Chittister, *The Gift of Years,* 4.

Bibliography

Abrams, M. H., ed. *The Norton Anthology of English Literature.* Vol. 2. New York: W. W. Norton & Company, 1962.

Achenbaum, W. Andrew. *Crossing Frontiers.* New York: Cambridge University Press, 1995.

———. *Old Age in the New Land.* Baltimore, Md.: Johns Hopkins University Press, 1978.

———. *Old Americans, Vital Communities.* Baltimore, Md.: Johns Hopkins University Press, 2005.

———. *Robert N. Butler, M.D.: Visionary of Healthy Aging.* New York: Columbia University Press, 2013.

———. *Shades of Gray: Old Age, American Values, and Federal Policies since 1920.* Boston: Little Brown, 1983.

———. *Social Security: Visions and Revisions.* New York: Cambridge University Press, 1986.

Anthony, Bolton. *Second Journeys: The Dance of Spirit in Later Life.* Chapel Hill, N.C.: Second Journeys Publications, 2013.

Atchley, Robert C. *Spirituality and Aging.* Baltimore, Md.: Johns Hopkins University Press, 2009.

Barks, Coleman, trans. and John Moyne, trans. *The Essential Rumi.* San Francisco: HarperSanFrancisco, 1995.

Barry, William, SJ "The Kingdom of God and Discernment." *America* 57(7) (1987): 157.

Becker, Ernst. *The Denial of Death*. New York: Free Press, 1973.

Bridges, Bill. *The Way of Transition: Embracing Life's Most Difficult Moments*. Reprint, New York: De Capo Press, 2001.

———. *Transitions: Making Sense of Life's Changes*. New York: Perseus Book Publishing, 1980.

Campbell, Joseph. *The Hero with a Thousand Faces*. San Rafael, Calif.: New World Library, 2008.

Camus, Albert. Quoted in Wit & Wisdom in *The Week* 13(641) (November 1, 2013): 15.

Carlin, George. Quoted in Wit & Wisdom in *The Week* 12(552) (February 10, 2012): 17.

Carlson, Richard. *Don't Sweat the Small Stuff and It's All Small Stuff: Simple Ways to Keep the Little Things from Taking Over Your Life*. New York: Hyperion, 1996.

Chittister, Joan. *The Gift of Years: Growing Older Gracefully*. New York: BlueBridge, 2008.

Cowley, Malcolm. *The View from 80*. New York: Viking Press, 1980.

Cox, Harvey. Interviewed by Sam Allis in "Finding Their Religion." Home/Lifestyle, *The Boston Globe*, June 3, 2011.

Cumming, Elaine, and William E. Henry. *Growing Old: The Process of Disengagement*. New York: Basic Books, 1961.

Davidson, Sara. *The December Project: An Extraordinary Rabbi and a Skeptical Seeker Confront Life's Greatest Mystery*. New York: HarperOne, 2014.

Dullea, Georgia. "Enough is Enough for Ex-Superwoman," *New York Times*, November 15, 1985.

Eliot, T. S. "The Four Quartets." In *T.S. Eliot: The Complete Poems and Plays, 1909–1950*. New York: Harcourt, Brace and World, 1952.

Erikson, Erik H. *The Life Cycle Completed: A Review*. New York: W. W. Norton & Company, 1982.

Erikson, Joan M. *Wisdom and the Senses: The Way of Creativity*. New York: W. W. Norton & Company, 1988.

Farrer-Halls, Gill. *The Illustrated Encyclopedia of Buddhist Wisdom.* Wheaton, Ill.: Theosophical Publishing House, 2000.

Farrow, Mia. Quoted in Wit & Wisdom in *The Week* 13(639) (October 18, 2013): 17.

Faulkner, William. "The Bear," *The Saturday Evening Post*, May 9, 1942.

Feinstein, David, and Stanley Krippner. *The Mythic Path: Discovering the Guiding Stories of Your Past—Creating a Vision for Your Future.* New York: Jeremy P. Tarcher, 1997.

———. *Personal Mythology: The Psychology of Your Evolving Self.* Los Angeles: Jeremy P. Tarcher, 1988.

Finley, James. *Merton's Palace of Nowhere: A Search for God through Awareness of the True Self.* Notre Dame, Ind.: Ave Maria Press, 1978.

Fischer, Kathleen. *Winter Grace: Spirituality and Aging.* Nashville: Upper Room Books, 1998.

Friedman, Rabbi Dayle. "Shever v'Tikkun/Shattering and Repair: Lessons from the Journey of Aging." Available online at http://zeek.forward.com/articles/117413/.

Goldman, Connie. *Who Am I . . . Now That I'm Not Who I Was? Conversations with Women in Mid-Life and the Years Beyond.* Minneapolis, Minn.: Nodin, 2009.

Gordon, Nancy. "In-the-Moment Connecting with Dementia Patients Reaps Rewards." *Aging Today: The Bimonthly Newspaper of the American Society on Aging*, May 30, 2013.

Guigo I. I. *Ladder of the Monks and Twelve Meditations.* Spencer, Mass.: Cistercian Publications, 1979.

Gunn, Robert Jingen. *Journey to Emptiness: Dogen, Merton, Jung and the Quest for Transformation.* Mahwah, N.J.: Paulist Press, 2000.

Haronian, Frank. "The Repression of the Sublime." *Synthesis* 1(1) (1974): 51–62.

Harter, Michael, SJ, ed. *Hearts on Fire: Praying with Jesuits.* Chicago: Loyola Press. 2004.

Havighurst, Robert J., and Ruth Albrecht. *Older People.* New York: Longmans, Green, and Company, 1953.

Havighurst, Robert J., Bernice L. Neugarten, and Sheldon S. Tobin. "Disengagement and Patterns of Aging." In *Middle Age and Aging: A Reader in Social Psychology,* edited by Bernice L. Neugarten. Chicago: The University of Chicago Press, 1968.

Heschel, Abraham Joshua. *I Asked for Wonder.* New York: Charles Scribner, 1954.

———. *Man's Quest for God,* New York: Charles Scribner, 1954.

———. *A Passion for Truth.* Woodstock, Vt.: Jewish Lights, 1995.

Hollis, James. *Finding Meaning in the Second Half of Life: How to Finally, Really Grow Up.* New York: Gotham Books, 2005.

Jacoby, Susan. *Never Say Die: The Myth and Marketing of the New Old Age.* New York: Pantheon Books, 2011.

Kabat-Zinn, Jon. *Wherever You Go, There You Are: Mindfulness Meditation in Everyday Life.* New York: Hyperion, 2005.

Keen, Sam. *Hymns to an Unknown God: Awakening the Spirit in Everyday Life.* Reissue, New York: Bantam Books, 1995.

Kohut, Heinz, and Ernest S. Wolf. "The Disorders of the Self and Their Treatment." In *Curative Factors in Dynamic Psychotherapy,* edited by Samuel Slipp, 44–59. New York: McGraw-Hill, 1982.

Kubler-Ross, Elisabeth, and Ira Byock. *On Death and Dying: What the Dying Have to Teach Doctors, Nurses, Clergy and Their Own Families.* New York: Scribner, 1969.

Kula, Irwin, and Linda Loewenthal. *Yearnings: Embracing the Sacred Messiness of Life.* New York: Hyperion, 2006.

Kuner, Susan, Carol Orsborn, Linda Quigley, and Karen Stroup. *Speak the Language of Healing: Living with Breast Cancer without Going to War.* Foreword by Jean Shinoda Bolen, M.D. Berkeley, Calif.: Conari Press, 1997.

Larson, Gary. *The Far Side Gallery 2.* New York, New York: Andrews, McMeel & Parker, 1986.

Lavelle, Louis. *The Dilemma of Narcissus.* Burdett, New York: Larson Publications, 1993.

Leiber, Jerry, and Mike Stoller. "Is That All There Is?" Recording released by Peggy Lee, 1969.

Lemon, B. W., V. L. Bengtson, and J. A. Peterson. "An Exploration of the Activity Theory of Aging: Activity Types and Life Satisfaction among In-Movers to a Retirement Community." *Journal of Gerontology* 27(4) (1972): 511–23.

Levinson, Daniel, with Charlotte Darrow, Edward Klein, Maria Levinson, and Braxton McKee. *The Seasons of a Man's Life.* New York: Alfred A. Knopf, 1978.

Lustbader, Wendy. *Life Gets Better: The Unexpected Pleasures of Growing Older.* New York: Jeremy P. Tarcher, 2011.

Lynch, William F., SJ *Christ and Apollo: The Dimensions of the Literary Imagination.* New York: Sheed & Ward, 1960.

Maddox, G. L. "Disengagement Theory: A Critical Evaluation." *The Gerontologist* 2 (1964): 80–83.

Maimonides, Moses. *Guide to the Perplexed.* Compiled by Michael Friedlander. New York: Cosimo Classics, 2007.

Malraux, Andre. *The Walnut Trees of Altenburg.* Chicago: Chicago University Press, 1992.

Martin, James, SJ. *Between Heaven and Mirth: Why Joy, Humor, and Laughter Are at the Heart of the Spiritual Life.* San Francisco: HarperOne, 2011.

May, Rollo. *The Courage to Create.* New York: W. W. Norton & Company, 1975.

———. *Freedom and Destiny.* New York: W. W. Norton & Company, 1981.

———. *Love and Will.* New York: W. W. Norton & Company, 1969.

McCartney, Paul. *Let It Be,* Apple Records. Recorded in 1969.

Mello, Anthony de, SJ. *Walking on Water.* New York: The Crossroad Publishing Company, 1998.

Merton, Thomas. *No Man Is an Island.* New York: Image/Doubleday, 1955.

——. *The Seven Storey Mountain.* New York: Harcourt, 1948.

——. *The Silent Life.* New York: Dell, 1957, and New York: Farrar, Strauss and Giroux, 1999.

Midler, Bette "What I Know Now," *AARP The Magazine,* online edition, September 21, 2012, www.aarp.org/entertainment/movies -for-grownups/info-09-2012/bette-midler-shares-life-lessons.html (accessed May 28, 2015).

Moody, Harry R. *Abundance of Life: Human Development Policies for an Aging Society.* New York: Columbia University Press, 1988.

——. *Aging: Concepts and Controversies,* 7th ed. Woburn, Mass.: Sage Publications, 2011.

——. "Conscious Aging: A New Level of Growth in Later Life." *Institute for Human Values in Aging Newsletter,* 2000.

——. *Ethics in an Aging Society.* Baltimore, Md.: Johns Hopkins University Press, 1992.

Moody, Harry R., and David Carroll. *The Five Stages of the Soul.* New York: Anchor Books, 1997.

Morgan, Richard L. *Remembering Your Story: Creating Your Own Spiritual Autobiography.* Nashville, Tenn.: Upper Room Books, 2002.

Neugarten, Bernice L., ed. *Middle Age and Aging: A Reader in Social Psychology.* Chicago: The University of Chicago Press, 1968.

Niebuhr, Reinhold. Quoted in *Grapevine: The International Journal of Alcoholics Anonymous,* January 1950, 6–7.

Nouwen, Henri J. M. *The Return of the Prodigal Son: A Story of Homecoming.* New York: Image Books, 1994.

Nouwen, Henri J. M., and Walter J. Gaffney. *Aging: The Fulfillment of Life.* New York: Image Books, 1976.

Orsborn, Carol. *The Art of Resilience: 100 Paths to Wisdom and Strength in an Uncertain World.* New York: Three Rivers Press, 1997.

——. *Enough is Enough: Exploding the Myth of Having it All.* New York: Putnam, 1986,

——. *Fierce with Age: Chasing God and Squirrels in Brooklyn.* Nashville, Tenn.: Turner Publishing, 2013.

———. *Nothing Left Unsaid: Words to Help You and Your Loved Ones through the Hardest Time.* Berkeley, Calif.: Conari Press, 2001.

———. *Solved by Sunset: The Self-Guided Intuitive Decision-Making Retreat.* New York: Harmony, 1996 and New York: Crown, 1997.

Puhl, Louis J., SJ. *The Spiritual Exercises of St. Ignatius.* Chicago: Loyola University Press, 1951.

Richmond, Lewis. *Aging as a Spiritual Practice: A Contemplative Guide to Growing Older and Wiser.* New York: Gotham Books, 2012.

Rilke, Rainer Maria. *Letters to a Young Poet.* New York: W. W. Norton & Company, 1954.

Rizzuto, Ana-Marie. *The Birth of the Living God: A Psychoanalytic Study.* Chicago: University of Chicago Press, 1979.

Robinson, John C. *The Three Secrets of Aging: A Radical Guide.* Winchester, UK: O-Books, 2012.

Rogala, Judith, and Carol Orsborn. *Trust, Inc.* Chicago: Ampersand, 2005.

Rohr, Richard. *Falling Upward: A Spirituality for the Two Halves of Life.* San Francisco: Jossey-Bass, 2011.

Roof, Wade Clark. *A Generation of Seekers: The Spiritual Journeys of the Baby Boom Generation.* San Francisco: HarperSanFrancisco, 1994.

———. *Spiritual Marketplace: Baby Boomers and the Remaking of American Religion.* Princeton, N.J.: Princeton University Press, 1999.

Roosevelt, Eleanor. Quoted in Wit & Wisdom in *The Week* 13(641) (November 1, 2013): 15.

Rumi, "The Guest House." In *The Essential Rumi.* Translated by Coleman Barks and John Moyne. San Francisco: HarperSanFrancisco, 1995.

Santayana, George. Quoted in Wit & Wisdom in *The Week* 13(641) (November 1, 2013): 15.

Sarton, May. *At Eighty-Two: A Journal.* New York: Norton, 1996.

———. "Riches Made of Loss" In *Collected Poems: 1930-1973.* New York: W. W. Norton & Company, 1974.

Schachter-Shalomi, Zalman. *From Age-ing to Sage-ing: A Profound New*

Vision of Growing Older. New York: Oxford University Press, 1997.

Schimmel, Solomon. *The Seven Deadly Sins: Jewish, Christian, and Classical Reflections on Human Psychology.* New York: Oxford University Press, 1997.

Scott-Maxwell, Florida. *The Measure of My Days: One Woman's Vivid, Enduring Celebration of Life and Aging.* New York: Penguin Books, 1968.

Senior, Thomas, and Cindy Senior. *The Joys of Getting Older.* Kansas City, Mo.: Andrews McMeel Publishing, 1999.

Sherman, Edmund. *Contemplative Aging: A Way of Being in Later Life.* New York: Gordian Knot Books, 2010.

Short, Robert L. *The Gospel According to Peanuts.* Richmond, Va.: John Knox Press, 1965.

Smull, Jimmy Laura, and Carol Orsborn. *The Silver Pearl: Our Generation's Journey to Wisdom.* Chicago: Ampersand, 2005.

Spielberg, Stephen. *The War Horse.* 2011.

Steinfels, Peter. "Conversations/Wade Clark Roof: Charting the Currents of Belief for the Generation That Rebelled." *New York Times,* May 30, 1993, Week in Review.

Teilhard de Chardin, Pierre. "Prayer for the Grace to Age Well." In Michael Harter, SJ, ed. *Hearts on Fire: Praying with Jesuits.* Chicago: Loyola Press, 2004.

Tennyson, Alfred, Lord. "Ulysses." In *The Norton Anthology of English Literature,* vol. 2., edited by M. H. Abrams, 736–37. New York: W.W. Norton & Company, 1962.

Thibault, Jane Marie. "Aging as a Natural Monastery." *Aging & Spirituality: Newsletter of the American Society on Aging's Forum on Religion, Spirituality and Aging.* San Francisco, 1996.

———. *A Deepening Love Affair: The Gift of God in Later Life.* Nashville, Tenn.: Upper Room Books, 1993.

Thibault, Jane Marie, and Richard L. Morgan. *Pilgrimage into the Last Third of Life: 7 Gateways to Spiritual Growth.* Nashville, Tenn.: Upper Room Books, 2012.

Thomas, Dylan. "Do not go gentle into that good night." In *In Country Sleep and Other Poems*. New York: New Directions, 1952.

Underhill, Evelyn. *The Mystic Way*. London: Forgotten Books, 2013.

———. *Practical Mysticism: A Little Book for Normal People*. New York: Dutton, 1943.

Vanier, Jean. *Community and Growth*. Mahwah, N.J.: Paulist Press, 1979/1989.

Weber, Robert. "Unraveling Projective Identification and Enactment." In *Complex Dilemmas in Group Therapy: Pathways to Resolution*, 2nd. ed., edited by Lise Motherwell and Joseph J. Shay, 71–83. New York: Routledge, 2014.

Weber, Robert, and Carol Orsborn. "The Question(s) of Age: Calling for a New Vision of Spiritual Aging." *Aging Today: The Bimonthly Newspaper of the American Society on Aging* (March–April 2013).

Weiselter, Leon. *Kaddish*. New York: Alfred A. Knopf, 1998.

Wilhelm, Hellmut, ed., and Cary F. Baynes, trans. *The I Ching*. Princeton, N.J.: Princeton University Press, 1967.

Yalom, Irvin D. *Staring at the Sun: Overcoming the Dread of Death*. San Francisco: Jossey-Bass, 2008.

Young-Eisendrath, Polly, and Melvin E. Miller. *The Psychology of Mature Spirituality: Integrity, Wisdom, Transcendence*. Philadelphia: Routledge, 2000.

About the Authors

ROBERT L. WEBER, PH.D.

Robert (Bob) L. Weber, Ph.D., a former Jesuit, is an assistant professor of psychology, part time, in the Department of Psychiatry at Harvard Medical School. He is the 2014 recipient of the American Society on Aging's FORSA Award (Forum on Religion, Spirituality and Aging) recognizing his leadership, locally and nationally, in exploring the role of spirituality and religion in the aging services field.

Following graduation with honors from Princeton University, Bob began a Master of Arts in Teaching degree program (M.A.T.) at Harvard University. After his first year of study and teaching in the Harvard program, he entered the New England Province of the Society of Jesus at the age of twenty-three. After the two-year Jesuit novitiate, Bob returned to Harvard, completed his M.A.T. degree, and then began and completed a three-year Master of Divinity degree with distinction in preparation for ordination as a priest.

Bob lived, worked, and trained as a Jesuit for almost ten years after which time, after much discernment, he decided to leave the order. In the meantime he had pursued doctoral training in clinical psychology at Temple University in Philadelphia. While there he studied with Diana Woodruff, a professor and protégée of James Birren, a preeminent gerontologist at USC. As the fruit of these studies, he wrote his master's thesis in psychology on "Value Changes and Adjustment in the Elderly."

Subsequently, Bob married and moved back to Boston, completing a predoctoral internship and postdoctoral fellowship at Massachusetts General Hospital-Harvard Medical School (MGH-HMS) and launching his career as a psychologist.

In the years following Bob immersed himself in psychoanalytic and psychodynamic theory and practice, while directing the group program at Cambridge Hospital-Harvard Medical School. In addition, he cofounded a group therapy practice, developed a new training program for the Northeastern Society for Group Psychotherapy (NSGP), and wrote the training manual for the American Group Psychotherapy Association (AGPA) and the National Register of Certified Group Psychotherapists (NRCGP).

When Bob entered his mid-fifties, he began a personal and professional journey intended to integrate the three major threads of his life: psychology, spirituality, and aging. Over time he became an active member of the American Society on Aging and served on the Leadership Council for the Forum on Religion, Spirituality and Aging. He began giving talks and leading workshops on spirituality, aging, and mental health across the country.

At the Massachusetts School of Professional Psychology (MSPP) Bob established a Conference on Spirituality, Aging, and Mental Health that is cosponsored by MSPP's Center for Mental Health and Aging and its Center for Psychotherapy and Spirituality. He serves the latter as an Advisory Board member.

He also served in an advisory capacity to the new spiritual outreach program of Somerville-Cambridge Elder Services.

Together with his colleague, Dr. Jane Marie Thibault, a gerontologist and Professor Emerita at the University of Louisville (KY) Medical School, Bob established a website and blog, www .ContemplAgeing.com, to disseminate ideas about the integration of spirituality, aging, and mental health. He also serves as coeditor with Carol Orsborn of www.SpiritualityofAge.com, the website based on this book.

CAROL ORSBORN, PH.D.

Carol Orsborn, Ph.D., earned her doctorate from Vanderbilt University, in the field of history and critical theory of religion, specializing in ritual studies and adult/spiritual development. She has authored over twenty-five books for and about quality of life for the boomer generation as they have progressed through multiple life stages over the past three decades. Her most recent book is titled *Fierce with Age: Chasing God and Squirrels in Brooklyn,* a memoir about her tumultuous year in which she transited "into the wild space beyond midlife." Her original work on resilience, based on her Random House book *The Art of Resilience: One Hundred Paths to Wisdom and Strength in an Uncertain World,* has been presented to such corporate clients as The Walt Disney Company, ABC Broadcast Network, and Wellpoint.

Carol is founder and editor in chief of Fierce with Age: The Digest of Boomer Wisdom, Inspiration & Spirituality, www .fiercewithage.com, and executive director of CoroFaith, an mHealth (mobile health) app that provides customized spiritual content to individuals from a broad range of religions. She has become a compelling voice of her generation, writing popular blogs for Huffington Post, PBS's "NextAvenue.org" and "Belief-Net.com." In addition to her writing about spirituality and aging, Carol writes a blog for individuals who resonate with her concept of becoming fierce with age and who have interest in Carol's keynotes and retreats: www.carolorsborn.com. She also serves as coeditor with Bob Weber of www.SpiritualityofAge .com, the website based on this book.

Carol has spoken before a number of association and industry groups, including multiple Book Expo Association conventions as panel chair of the Marketing to Boomer Women session, American Society of Aging, What's Next Boomer Summit, the Positive Aging Conference, and many more. She is frequently interviewed by the press, speaking on behalf of the boomer generation.

In the late 1980s Carol started "Superwomen's Anonymous." The group hit a nerve, winning coverage in *The New York Times, The Today Show,* and *Oprah,* among others. News of her organization, followed by her first book, *Enough is Enough: Exploding the Myth of Having It All* was credited as a progenitor of both the simplicity and work/life balance movements. More than twenty-five books followed, chronicling the challenges her generation of men and women have faced and the stereotypes they've defied as they've transited from early parenthood through midlife crisis and beyond.

Carol, a Phi Beta Kappa graduate of UC Berkeley, received her Master's of Theological Studies from Vanderbilt University Divinity School. She has done postgraduate work in spiritual guidance at Stillpoint and the Spirituality Center at Mount St. Mary's College in Los Angeles and the New Seminary of Interfaith Studies in Manhattan. Teaching ethics, leadership, and resilience, she has served on the faculties of Georgetown University, Vanderbilt University's Leadership Development Center of the Owen Graduate School of Management, Loyola Marymount University, and the Doctoral Program in Organizational Leadership at Pepperdine University's Graduate School of Education and Psychology.

Carol, a mother and grandmother, lives on the Cumberland River in Madison, Tennessee, with her husband, Dan, and their dogs, Lucky and Molly.

Invitation to Stay Connected

We invite you to visit the website for this book,
www.SpiritualityofAge.com,
where you will find:

- Links to Bob Weber's and Carol Orsborn's blogs and updates
- Free reading and discussion guides for book club members
- A calendar of upcoming events
- Spiritual exercises
- Connections to the authors' social media presence on Facebook, Twitter, and LinkedIn

For information about speaking and retreat opportunities
with the coauthors, contact Bob Weber at:
Bob@SpiritualityofAge.com

You are also invited to visit the authors' individual websites as listed on page 233.

CAROL ORSBORN

www.FierceWithAge.com
(The Digest of Boomer Wisdom, Inspiration and Spirituality)
    Free monthly online digest and daily updates of the best content about spirituality and aging for boomers

www.CarolOrsborn.com
Carol Orsborn's personal blog about aging as a spiritual path

Carol Orsborn can be contacted at: **Carol@fiercewithage.com**

BOB WEBER

www.Contemplageing.com
Jane Marie Thibault and Bob Weber's website and blog, disseminating ideas about the integration of spirituality, aging, and mental health

Bob Weber can be contacted at: **Bob@SpiritualityofAge.com**

BOOKS OF RELATED INTEREST

Herbs for Healthy Aging
Natural Prescriptions for Vibrant Health
by David Hoffmann, FNIMH, AHG

The Healing Intelligence of Essential Oils
The Science of Advanced Aromatherapy
by Kurt Schnaubelt, Ph.D.

Natural Remedies for Inflammation
by Christopher Vasey, N.D.

The Yin Yoga Kit
The Practice of Quiet Power
by Biff Mithoefer

Yoga for Cancer
A Guide to Managing Side Effects, Boosting Immunity, and
Improving Recovery for Cancer Survivors
by Tari Prinster

The Science and Practice of Humility
The Path to Ultimate Freedom
by Jason Gregory

Walking Your Blues Away
How to Heal the Mind and Create Emotional Well-Being
by Thom Hartmann

Fight Alzheimer's with Vitamins and Antioxidants
by Kedar N. Prasad, Ph.D.

INNER TRADITIONS • BEAR & COMPANY
P.O. Box 388
Rochester, VT 05767
1-800-246-8648
www.InnerTraditions.com

Or contact your local bookseller